Taste of Joy

And a Little Bit of Chocolate

Official
Cookbook of
Women of Joy

256-355-1554
www.philwaldrep.org
PHIL WALDREP MINISTRIES
Trinity, Alabama

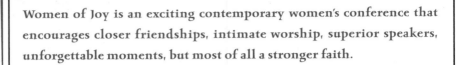

Women of Joy is an exciting contemporary women's conference that encourages closer friendships, intimate worship, superior speakers, unforgettable moments, but most of all a stronger faith.

Copyright © 2010

Phil Waldrep Ministries
P.O. Box 148
Trinity, Alabama 35673

First Printing   April 2010

ISBN 978-0-9713746-3-8

Copies of "Taste of Joy and a Little Bit of Chocolate" may be obtained by calling 1-800-374-1550 or www.womenofjoy.org

Cover design by Ruth Bochte and Debbie Waldrep

WIMMER
COOKBOOKS

A CONSOLIDATED GRAPHICS COMPANY

800.548.2537   wimmerco.com

Introduction

Taste of Joy and a Little Bit of Chocolate is a fresh new way to make cooking a fun and exciting time for you and your friends!

This cookbook will inspire you to reach out to others, as you scroll through the pages, find a dish or a dessert that you would like to prepare, and then invite some friends over to share it with you. The fun and fellowship will give you memories to last a lifetime.

Women of Joy is about new beginnings, new friendships, and spending time with your family.

In this cookbook you will find new recipes and some old favorites. Many are easy and quick to prepare, making your busy life a little easier.

In our busy lives we tend to forget how important it is to sit down and eat a meal together. It is our prayer that this cookbook will cause you to cook and share with the people you love.

Blessings,

Phil & Debbie Waldrep
Phil Waldrep Ministries
Trinity, Alabama

Cookbook Committee

Ruth Bochte

Emily Bryan

Paige Betterton

Karen Carnes

Penny Owens

Sherree Roberts

Debbie Waldrep

Acknowledgement

To all the "Women of Joy" who watch the food channels
and say, "I could do that" but never do... Here's your chance!

Table of Contents

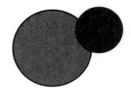

This book is dedicated to our children:
Maegan, Melodi, Zach,
Courtney and Lucas.
May they be forever blessed
with great friends, great food,
and truly blessed by our
Great God!

Taste of Appetizers & Beverages

Sausage Balls

1   pound hot or mild sausage
1   (8 ounce) package shredded sharp
      Cheddar cheese

3   cups biscuit baking mix

Mix sausage, cheese and biscuit baking mix. Form into small balls. Bake 350 degrees for 20 minutes, or until they are golden brown.

Sausage Apple Balls

1   pound bulk pork sausage
1   cup chopped raisins
½   cup chopped walnuts

2   cups biscuit mix
1   cup grated apple
½   teaspoon apple pie spice

Combine all ingredients. Shape into 1 inch balls. Bake on ungreased cookie sheet at 350 degrees for 20 minutes.

Spinach Squares

½ stick margarine
½ onion, finely chopped
8 ounces fresh sliced mushrooms
4 eggs, beaten
¼ cup breadcrumbs
1 can cream of mushroom soup
¼ cup grated Parmesan cheese
⅛ teaspoon pepper, oregano, basil
2 (10 ounce) packages chopped frozen spinach, thawed and drained

Sauté margarine with onions and mushrooms. Combine rest of ingredients with onion and mushroom mixture. Place in greased 9x13 inch baking dish. Bake at 325 degrees for 20 to 25 minutes. Cut into squares.

Ham Roll Ups

1 package ham slices
1 (8 ounce) package cream cheese, softened
1 green onion for each ham slice

Clean and cut tops off onions. Spread cream cheese on ham slices. Add one onion to each slice and roll up. Wrap in wax paper and refrigerate until serving time. Unwrap and slice into ½ to 1 inch pieces.

Halftime Special

2 cans diced tomatoes with jalapeños
1 can black beans, drained and rinsed
1 can whole kernel corn, drained
1 medium onion, chopped
½ bunch cilantro, chopped
½ lime, juiced
   garlic fresh chopped or powder to taste

Combine ingredients and serve with tortilla chips.

Candied Bacon Knots

1   cup brown sugar   1   pound thinly sliced bacon

Preheat oven to 350 degrees. Line a broiler pan with foil. Place broiler rack over foil and coat with a nonstick cooking spray. Put brown sugar in a shallow dish. Cut bacon pieces in half. Cross one end of the bacon over the other to form a V. Press one side of bacon into the brown sugar, coating well. Arrange knots in a single layer, sugar side up, on the prepared broiler rack. Bake 15 to 20 minutes or until bacon is crisp and sugar is bubbly. Drain and cool on cooling racks, sugar side up. Can be made up to 3 hours ahead and held at room temperature.

Party Quiche Bites

2   tablespoons butter or margarine
1   cup dry breadcrumbs, divided
½   cup (1 stick) butter or margarine
1   cup chopped onion
2   cloves garlic, crushed (1 teaspoon)
4   slices white sandwich bread
⅔   cup milk (for soaking)
1   (20 ounce) package frozen,
      chopped broccoli, thawed

1   (8 ounce) package cream cheese,
      softened
4   large eggs
1   teaspoon salt
    dash of hot sauce
¼   teaspoon pepper
2   cups (8 ounces) grated sharp
      Cheddar cheese

Preheat oven to 350 degrees. Prepare a 15x10x1 inch baking pan by greasing with 2 tablespoons butter and dusting with ½ cup breadcrumbs. Set aside. Melt the stick of butter in a large skillet; add onion and garlic and cook until soft. Remove from pan and set aside. Soak the bread in milk and set aside. Place broccoli in skillet used to cook onions and cook over low heat, just long enough to completely dry broccoli, being careful not to scorch. Remove from pan and finely chop. In a large mixing bowl, beat the cream cheese until smooth and light. Add the eggs, one at a time, mixing well. Add the onions and garlic with their butter, the soaked bread (with liquid), dry broccoli and a dash of hot sauce. Mix thoroughly and season with salt and pepper; taste and adjust seasoning if necessary. Pour into prepared pan. Sprinkle evenly with the cheddar cheese, and remaining ½ cup breadcrumbs. Bake 20 to 30 minutes or until set and puffed in middle. Remove from oven and allow to cool completely until firm.

Cheese Straws

1	pound sharp Cheddar cheese, grated	2	cups flour
½	cup butter or margarine, softened		salt to taste
			red pepper to taste

Combine grated cheese and softened butter in a bowl. Work in flour, salt, and pepper using hands. Mix well. Place mixture in a pastry bag and make different shapes. Be creative.

Gala Pecan Dip

1	(8 ounce) package cream cheese	½	teaspoon garlic salt
2	tablespoons milk	¼	teaspoon black pepper
1	(8 ounce) package sliced beef, finely chopped	½	cup sour cream
		½	cup chopped pecans
¼	cup chopped green pepper	2	tablespoons butter
2	tablespoons dehydrated onion flakes (can use fresh)	½	teaspoon salt

Combine cream cheese and milk; mix until well blended. Add beef, green peppers, onion, garlic salt, and black pepper mixing well. Fold in sour cream; spoon into baking dish. Heat pecans in melted butter and salt; sprinkle over cream cheese mixture. Bake at 350 degrees for 20 minutes. Serve hot with crackers.

> God calls us to rise above our
> circumstances, and sometimes
> He even tells us to change
> those circumstances.
> Don't be afraid to step out in faith.

Little Smokies

1   package little smokies   1   bottle barbeque sauce

Pour sauce in the crock pot. Add little smokies and cook for 30 minutes on high. Serve hot.

Bacon Wrapped Pigs

1   package hotdogs   2   cups brown sugar
1   package bacon

Cut hotdogs in ⅓ pieces. Wrap bacon around each piece and secure with toothpick. Place in the crock pot, pour brown sugar over hotdogs. Cook for 1 hour on high. Serve warm.

Party Ham Ball

1   (8 ounce) package cream cheese   1   bunch chopped green onions
2   packages thin sliced ham, chopped   chopped pecans

Combine all together and roll in chopped pecans. Serve with crackers.

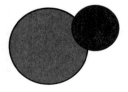

Buffalo Chicken Dip

4 boneless chicken breast halves, boiled and shredded
1 (12 ounce) bottle hot sauce
2 (8 ounce) packages cream cheese
1 (16 ounce) bottle Ranch dressing
8 ounces Monterey Jack cheese or Cheddar cheese grated

Combine the shredded chicken meat with the entire bottle of hot sauce. In a saucepan, combine the cream cheese, other cheeses, and ranch dressing over medium heat until smooth. Mix this well with the chicken. Pour mixture into 9x13 inch baking pan. Bake uncovered at 350 degrees for 30 to 40 minutes or until bubbly. Watch that the top doesn't get browned. Let stand 10 minutes. Serve hot or warm with Doritos or Fritos scoops.

Eight Layer Tex-Mex Dip

1 pound hamburger meat
1 package taco seasoning mix
1 (16 ounce) can fat free refried beans
½ cup chunky salsa
1 cup fat free sour cream
1 cup shredded taco cheese
2 medium tomatoes, chopped
1 avocado, peeled and diced
¼ cup sliced green onions
2 tablespoons chopped black olives
   baked tortilla chips

Brown hamburger meat and taco seasoning in skillet, drain and set aside. In a medium bowl, stir together the beans and salsa. Spread the bean mixture on a 9 inch platter or in a pie plate. Spread the sour cream on top of the bean layer. Spread the hamburger mixture on top of the sour cream layer. Then layer the shredded cheese, tomatoes, avocado, green onions, and olives on top. Cover and refrigerate for up to 4 hours. Serve with tortilla chips.

Doo-Dads

1	box pretzel sticks	3	teaspoons salt seasoning
1	box corn snacks	1	box toasted whole grain oat cereal
2	sticks margarine, melted	1	box rice or corn square cereal
3	teaspoons soy sauce	1	pound pecans or mixed nuts
3	teaspoons garlic powder		

Place first 6 ingredients in a large pan and mix well. Add the cereal and nuts and bake at 200 degrees for 2 hours. Stir occasionally.

Pineapple Cheese Dip

2	(8 ounce) packages cream cheese, softened	¼	cup chopped green bell peppers
		½	cup chopped pecans
1	small can crushed pineapple	1	tablespoon seasoned salt

Combine all ingredients including the pineapple juice. If you would prefer to make a cheese ball, just drain the pineapple juice, chill, then roll the ball in the chopped nuts. Best served with butter-flavored crackers.

Creamy Spinach Dip

1	cup mayonnaise	1	(10 ounce) package frozen chopped spinach, thawed
1	package vegetable mix	1	(16 ounce) container sour cream

Squeeze liquid out of spinach. Combine all ingredients. Chill for 2 hours. Serve with assorted crackers or vegetables.

Sausage Pinwheels

2 cups plain flour
⅓ cup cornmeal
1 teaspoon baking powder
½ teaspoon salt

4 tablespoons shortening
1 pound pork sausage
milk

Mix the flour, cornmeal, baking powder, salt, shortening, and enough milk to make a stiff dough. Roll it out flat and then spread the sausage over the top of the dough. Roll it up and slice thin. Place the thin slices on a cookie sheet and bake in the oven at 400 degrees for 15 minutes. Take out and let cool.

Shrimp Dip

½ pint sour cream
1 (8 ounce) package cream cheese
½ cup finely chopped celery
½ cup finely chopped or diced onions
1 lemon, juiced

2 cans small shrimp
dash salt and pepper to taste
granulated garlic powder to taste
red pepper to taste

Combine sour cream with cream cheese. Add celery, onions, salt, pepper, lemon juice, granulated garlic powder, and cayenne to taste. Mash the shrimp with a fork and add to cheese mixture. Sprinkle red pepper on top. Refrigerate overnight preferably. Can also be served immediately. Makes approximately 1 quart.

My husband gave me a mood ring
the other day. When I'm in a good mood,
it turns green; when I'm in a bad mood,
it leaves a red mark on his forehead.

Spring Dip

1 (8 ounce) package cream cheese
¼ cup finely chopped onion
¼ cup finely ground pecans
salt to taste

Thoroughly combine and eat with fancy crackers.

Chocolate Chip Cheese Ball

1 (8 ounce) package cream cheese, softened
½ cup butter, softened
¼ teaspoon vanilla extract
¾ cup confectioners' sugar
2 tablespoons brown sugar
¾ cup miniature semisweet chocolate chips
¾ cup finely chopped pecans

Beat together the cream cheese, butter, and vanilla until fluffy. Gradually add sugars, beating just until combined. Stir in chocolate chips. Cover and refrigerate for 2 hours. Place the cream cheese mixture on a large piece of plastic wrap. Then shape into ball and roll in pecans.

Cheese Ball

1 (8 ounce) package cream cheese
8 ounces grated Cheddar cheese
1 tablespoon grated pimento
1 tablespoon grated onion
1 tablespoon Worcestershire sauce
1 tablespoon lemon juice
½ cup finely chopped pecans

Bring the cream cheese to room temperature. Mix remaining ingredients except pecans. Roll in chopped pecans. Wrap and chill.

Fruit Dip

1   pint sour cream
1   tablespoon brown sugar

1   teaspoon vanilla extract

Mix all ingredients and serve in side dish for dipping mixed fruit or mixed with fruit for dessert.

Pecan Sandwiches

1   (8 ounce) package cream cheese
     with onions and chives

1   cup finely chopped pecans
2   teaspoons Worcestershire sauce

Mix all ingredients, spread on bread and cut into desired shapes.

Roasted Pecans

1   stick margarine
7   cups pecan halves

1   tablespoon garlic salt

Preheat oven to 350 degrees. Melt margarine in a 9x13 inch pan. Add pecans. Stir to coat well. Sprinkle on garlic salt. Bake for 30 minutes, stirring every 10 minutes.

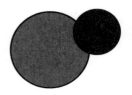

Stuffed Mushrooms

20	medium mushrooms	14	Ritz crackers, finely crushed
3	tablespoons butter	2	tablespoons grated Parmesan cheese
2	tablespoons finely chopped onions	½	teaspoon Italian seasoning
2	tablespoons finely chopped red peppers		

Preheat oven to 400 degrees. Remove stems from mushrooms. Finely chop enough of the stems to measure ¼ cup, set aside. Cover and refrigerate remaining stems for other use. Melt butter in large skillet on medium heat. Add ¼ cup chopped mushroom stems, the onions and peppers; cook and stir until vegetables are tender. Stir in cracker crumbs, cheese and Italian seasoning. Spoon crumb mixture evenly into mushroom caps. Place on ungreased baking sheet. Bake 15 minutes or until heated through.

Sweet Fruit Sandwiches

2	(8 ounce) packages cream cheese, softened	1	(10 ounce) jar maraschino cherries, cut up and drained on paper towels
1	(15 ounce) can crushed pineapple, drained	7	tablespoons confectioners' sugar
		¾	cup finely chopped pecans
		2	king sized loaves of bread

Mix all ingredients then refrigerate for several hours or overnight. Trim crust from bread. Spread filling thinly on one side of a slice of bread. Place another slice on top. Cut corner to corner each way making 4 triangles from each sandwich. Wrap and refrigerate if not serving immediately. This is enough filling for 2 king-size loaves of bread.

Pinwheels

2	(8 ounce) packages cream cheese		6	green onions
1	(4 ounce) can black olives, sliced		2	(4 ounce) jars jalapeños
1	(4 ounce) jar pimentos		4	(12 inch) tortillas
1	package ranch dressing			

Mix all ingredients except tortillas. Spread on tortillas and roll into a log. Cut into ¼ inch slices and refrigerate for 1 hour.

Stuffed Wonton Shells

1	pound sausage, cooked and drained		1	small can chopped black olives
1	cup shredded Cheddar cheese		1	cup ranch dressing
1	cup grated Monterey Jack cheese		1	package wonton shells

Mix all ingredients together. Place shells in muffin pans and bake at 350 degrees until lightly browned. Spoon mixture into shells and bake for an additional 10 minutes.

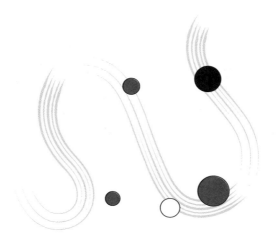

Easy Cheesy Bean Dip

1 (16 ounce) can refried beans
1 (10½ ounce) can Cheddar cheese

1 (10 ounce) can diced tomatoes and green chilies, undrained

Combine all ingredients and heat thoroughly. Serve warm with tortilla chips.

Puppy Chow

1 (12 ounce) bag chocolate chips
1 (12 ounce) jar peanut butter

1 small box Rice Chex cereal
½ box powdered sugar

Melt peanut butter and chocolate chips on the stove top. Remove from heat and stir in cereal. Pour this mix into a brown bag. Add powdered sugar and shake to coat all pieces evenly. Store in a ziploc bag or plastic container.

Fried Dill Pickles

3 cups and 2 tablespoons flour, divided
1 large egg
½ cup milk
1 drop hot sauce

1 teaspoon salt
1 teaspoon pepper
¼ teaspoon garlic salt
sliced dill pickles
vegetable oil for frying

Whisk together 2 tablespoons flour, egg, milk and hot sauce. In a separate bowl, sift together 3 cups flour, salt, pepper and garlic salt. Dip pickle slices in egg mixture, then in flour mixture. Fry in 3 inches of oil until lightly browned. Drain on paper towel.

Fluffy Cream Cheese Dip (for strawberries)

1 (8 ounce) package cream cheese, softened
2 cups powdered sugar
2 teaspoons vanilla extract
1 cup whipped cream
fresh whole strawberries

Beat cream cheese, powdered sugar and vanilla at medium speed with an electric mixer until fluffy. Fold in whipped cream. Serve with fresh strawberries.

Orange–Nut Sandwiches

2 (8 ounce) packages cream cheese, softened
¼ cup grated orange rind
1 cup chopped dark raisins
½ cup chopped pecans
1 (6 ounce) can orange juice concentrate, thawed
4 tablespoons powdered sugar
whole wheat bread

Mix together cream cheese, orange rind, raisins, pecans, orange juice and powdered sugar. Spread on whole-wheat bread. Cut into "fingers."

Guacamole Dip

2 avocados, scooped and coarsely chopped
1 lime
½ small onion, diced
1 clove garlic, diced
1 jalapeño, diced (remove ribs and seeds)
¼ cup cilantro, chopped
1 tablespoon sour cream
¼ package sweetener
salt
tortilla chips

Place chopped avocados in bowl. Squeeze lime juice over avocado. Add onion, garlic, jalapeño, cilantro and sour cream. Mix well. Season to taste with sweetener and salt. Serve with tortilla chips.

BLT Dip

2   cans Rotel tomatoes, well drained
1   cup mayonnaise
8   ounces cream cheese, softened
1   cup sour cream
1   jar bacon bits
    chips

Mix tomatoes, mayonnaise, cream cheese, sour cream and bacon bits well. Serve with chips.

BLT Stuffed Tomatoes

2   pints cherry tomatoes
½   cup mayonnaise
1   chipotle chile in adobo sauce, finely chopped
    salt
    pepper
1   cup finely chopped romaine lettuce
6   slices bacon, cooked crisp and crumbled

Cut ends of tomatoes off. With small end of melon baler, scoop out insides of tomatoes. Mix mayonnaise, chile, salt and pepper together. Put lettuce in tomato. Add mayonnaise mixture and top with bacon.

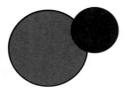

Redneck Caviar

2 cans black-eyed peas, drained
2 cans shoepeg corn, drained
2 cans Rotel tomatoes, drained
1 can large diced tomatoes
1 can black beans, drained
1 bell pepper

cilantro to taste
6 green onions, chopped
1 small onion, chopped
1 (16 ounce) bottle zesty Italian
dressing

Mix all ingredients and refrigerate overnight. Serve with chips or crackers. This mix gets better everyday.

Mocha Punch

1 cup water
1 cup sugar
2 tablespoons instant coffee

1 quart vanilla ice cream
1 quart chocolate ice cream
5 cups milk

Bring water and sugar to a boil to make a syrup. Add coffee. Cool. This may be made ahead and kept in refrigerator for 7 to 10 days. Mix syrup with both flavors or ice cream and the milk. Punch should be the consistency of a shake.

Good communication is as
stimulating as black coffee,
and just as hard to sleep after.

Tea Punch

1	cup sugar	4	cups pineapple juice
1	cup strong brewed tea	4	cups prepared lemonade
4	cups orange juice	1	(2 liter) bottle ginger ale, chilled

In a pitcher, combine sugar and tea. Stir until sugar is dissolved. Stir in orange juice, pineapple juice and lemonade. Chill in refrigerator for 4 hours. Just before serving, pour chilled juice mixture into a punch bowl and stir in ginger ale.

Orange Julius

1	cup orange juice	¾	teaspoon vanilla extract
1	cup water	¼	cup granulated sugar
2	egg whites	1	heaping cup ice

Combine all ingredients in a blender set on high speed for 30 seconds. Serves 2.

Coffee Punch

1	quart strong coffee	2	quarts vanilla ice cream
5	teaspoons sugar	1	(16 ounce) container Cool Whip
5	teaspoons vanilla extract		

Make coffee and let it cool to lukewarm. Add sugar and vanilla. Pour into punch bowl. Spoon in ice cream and Cool Whip. Stir. Serve immediately.

Sparkling Homemade Lemonade

3 cups water	¾ cup sugar
½ cup freshly squeezed lemon juice	lemon slices

Combine water, lemon juice and sugar in 2 quart pitcher; mix well. Pour into tall ice-filled glasses. Garnish with lemon slices. Makes 4 servings.

Hot Mocha Mix

1 cup cocoa	2 cups instant non-fat dry milk
½ cup instant coffee powder	2 cups sugar
2 cups non-dairy creamer	

Mix and keep in covered jar. To serve, place 2 ½ teaspoons or more to suit taste in a cup. Add boiling water and stir well. Top with marshmallow, if desired.

Cranberry Tea

1 gallon water	1 (6 ounce) box cherry Jell-O
3 cups sugar	1 quart apple juice
3 family-size tea bags	1 quart cranberry juice
3 cinnamon sticks	1 cup lemon juice
1 teaspoon whole cloves	1 (6 ounce) can frozen orange juice

Boil water, remove from heat and add sugar. Add tea bags and let stand for 6 minutes. Remove tea bags and add cinnamon sticks and cloves; let stand 30 minutes. Remove spices and add Jell-O, apple juice, cranberry juice, lemon juice and orange juice. Makes 1½ gallons.

Applewood Julep

1   cup pineapple juice
1   cup orange juice

¼   cup lemon juice
1   quart apple juice

Mix all juices together in a pitcher and refrigerate.

Chocolate Milk Shake

2-3   scoops vanilla ice cream
⅔   cups milk

2   tablespoons chocolate syrup

Beat ingredients with mixer or put into shaker and shake thoroughly.

Hot Chocolate Mix

1 (2 pound) can Nestlé Quick
1 (1 pound) box confectioners' sugar
1 (16 ounce) jar Coffee Mate
1 (9.6 ounce) box powdered milk

Mix all ingredients. Store in covered container. When ready to use, add ½ cup of mix to 1 cup water.

Percolator Punch

2¼ cups pineapple juice
1¾ cups water
2 cups cranberry juice
1 tablespoon whole cloves
½ teaspoon whole allspice
3 sticks cinnamon, broken
¼ teaspoon salt
½ cup brown sugar

Pour juices and water in electric percolator. Put remaining ingredients in basket. Perk for 10 minutes until spices permeate. Serve hot. Makes 8 to 10 servings.

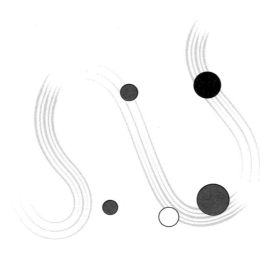

Wassail

2 quarts sweet apple cider
2 cups pineapple juice
1½ cups orange juice
¾ cup lemon juice

1 cup granulated sugar
2 sticks whole cinnamon
1 teaspoon whole cloves

Combine ingredients and bring to a boil. Serve hot.

Iced Coffee

1 quart vanilla ice cream, softened
¼ cup sugar
¾ teaspoon nutmeg
3 cups milk

1 teaspoon vanilla extract
8 cups brewed coffee, room
    temperature

Mix all ingredients together in punch bowl.

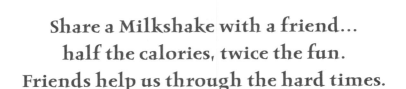

Share a Milkshake with a friend...
half the calories, twice the fun.
Friends help us through the hard times.

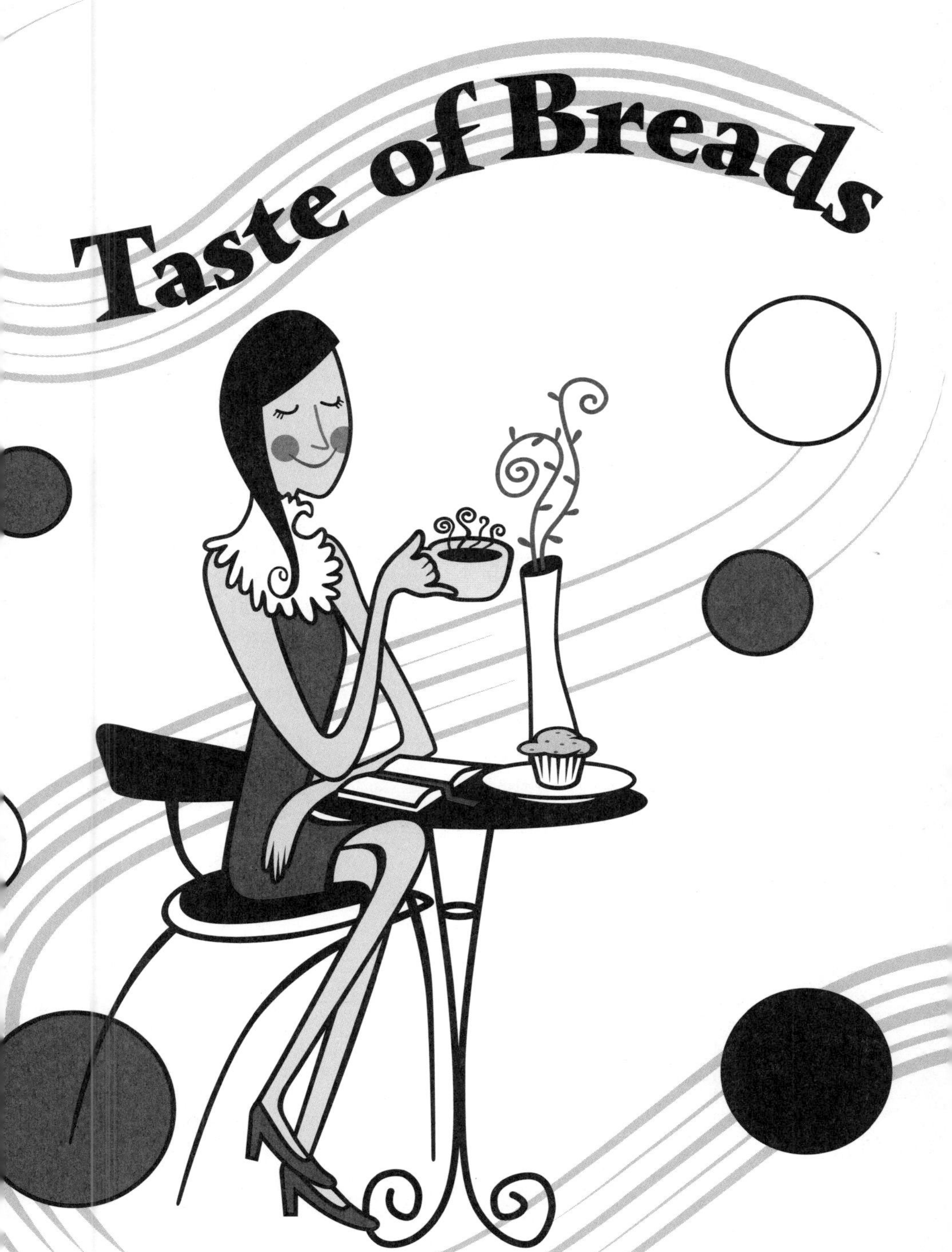
Taste of Breads

Sweet Potato Bread

¾	cup oil	½	teaspoon nutmeg
1	cup sugar	½	teaspoon cinnamon
2	eggs	¾	cup raw grated sweet potatoes
3	tablespoons milk	¾	cup pecans or walnuts
1½	cups self-rising flour	½	teaspoon vanilla extract

Preheat oven to 350 degrees. Grease loaf pan and line with wax paper. In a mixing bowl, mix oil, sugar, milk and eggs together. Add flour, nutmeg, cinnamon and fold in sweet potatoes and nuts. Add vanilla. Pour into loaf pan. Bake 45 minutes.

Chocolate Macadamia Bread

2	ounces unsweetened chocolate	2	teaspoons vanilla extract
2	cups self-rising flour	1	teaspoon almond extract
1¼	cups sugar	1¼	cups buttermilk
⅓	cup oil	½	cup finely chopped macadamia
2	eggs		nuts

Melt chocolate in a double boiler on stove and set aside. Mix all ingredients together in order. Pour into greased loaf pan. Bake at 350 degrees for 45 minutes.

MATTHEW 6:11

Give us today our daily bread.

Cheddar Garlic Biscuits

2 cups biscuit baking mix
⅔ cup milk
½ cup shredded Cheddar cheese

2 tablespoons melted butter
⅛ teaspoon garlic powder

Heat oven to 450 degrees. Mix biscuit mix, milk and cheese to form soft dough. Drop by spoonfuls onto ungreased cookie sheet. Bake 8 to 10 minutes. Mix butter and garlic powder and brush over warm biscuits.

Banana Nut Bread

1 box yellow cake mix
1 teaspoon baking soda
1 cup canola oil

2 cups mashed bananas
1 cup chopped pecans
3 eggs

Preheat oven to 325 degrees. Combine all ingredients and pour into a tube pan or 2 loaf pans. Bake for 1 hour in tube pan or for 45 minutes if using 2 loaf pans.

Betty's Salsa Cornbread

½ cups cornmeal
½ teaspoon garlic powder
1½ tablespoon vegetable oil
1 (4 ounce) can diced green chilies, drained

½ cup milk
1 egg, lightly beaten
½ cup salsa

Mix oil, chilies, egg, milk and salsa. Add cornmeal and garlic powder, stir just until blended. Pour in greased preheated pan. Bake 35 minutes at 425 degrees.

Banana Nut Bread

3 cups flour
2 cups sugar
1 teaspoon soda
1 teaspoon salt
1 teaspoon cinnamon
1 teaspoon vanilla extract

1 cup chopped nuts
3 eggs
1½ cups oil
2 cups mashed bananas
1 small can crushed pineapple, drained

Combine dry ingredients. Combine liquid ingredients. Mix well. Grease 2 (9x5 inch) loaf pans. Pour in pans and bake 1 hour at 350 degrees. Let cool in pan 10 minutes before removing.

Harold's Corn Bread

1½ cups cornmeal
¾ cup oil
2 eggs
1 small can cream corn

1 (8 ounce) container sour cream
1 small chopped onion
dash of salt

Mix all ingredients in bowl. Pour into preheated pan and bake at 450 degrees for 30 minutes.

Monkey Bread in a Bag

3 cans biscuits, quartered
1 cup sugar
1 cup brown sugar

2 teaspoons cinnamon
1 cup chopped nuts
3 sticks butter

Mix sugars, cinnamon and nuts and place in brown paper bag. Take the biscuits and drop them into the bag. Melt the butter, and drop in on biscuits. Shake well. Pour biscuits into a greased Bundt pan. Bake at 400 degrees for 20 minutes.

May substitute gallon ziploc bag for paper bag.

Hot Rolls

1	cup shortening	2	cakes yeast
1	cup sugar	1	cup cold water
1½	teaspoons salt	6	cups unsifted flour
1	cup boiling water	2	eggs, beaten

Pour boiling water over salt, shortening and sugar. Blend. Add eggs. Dissolve yeast in the cup of cold water. Add to mixture. Add flour, blending well. Cover, place in refrigerator. Make into rolls as desired and brush with melted butter. Let rise in a warm place and bake at 425 degrees for 20 minutes, or until lightly browned.

Quick Rolls

1	cup self-rising flour	¼	cup mayonnaise
½	cup milk		

Mix all ingredients and drop into hot greased muffin tins. Bake at 450 degrees oven for 12 to 15 minutes or until brown. Makes 6 large or 12 small muffins.

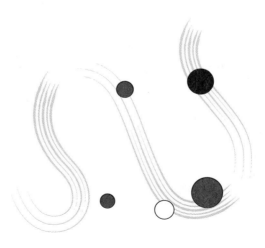

Piña Colada Bread

1   box pineapple cake mix
2   eggs
½   cup oil

1   cup water
1   cup coconut
1   cup chopped pecans

Mix all ingredients together. Pour into 2 loaf pans. Bake at 350 degrees for 25 to 30 minutes.

Hush Puppies

2   cups cornmeal
1   tablespoon flour
1   tablespoon soda
1   tablespoon baking powder

1   tablespoon salt
6   tablespoons chopped onion
1   egg, beaten
1   cup buttermilk

Mix and sift all dry ingredients. Add chopped onion. Combine the beaten egg with the milk. Add to dry ingredients. Drop by spoonfuls into deep, hot grease. When done, hush puppies will float. Put on brown paper and drain. Makes 36 to 48 small hush puppies.

Stuffed French Bread

1   loaf French bread
1   (8 ounce) container sour cream
1   (16 ounce) package shredded
      Cheddar cheese

½   cup chopped ham
1   chopped bell pepper
1   teaspoon steak sauce

Hull out loaf of bread. Combine all ingredients, including crumbs from bread. Spoon back into loaf of bread. Wrap in aluminum foil. Bake at 350 degrees for 1 hour.

Strawberry Bread

3 cups self-rising flour
2 cups sugar
2 (10 ounce) packages frozen
   strawberries, reserve ½ cup juice
   for spread

1 cup oil
4 eggs, beaten
1 (8 ounce) package cream cheese,
   softened

Mix all ingredients, except strawberry juice and cream cheese. Pour batter into 2 well-greased loaf pans. Bake at 325 degrees for 1 hour. Blend cream cheese with reserved strawberry juice. Spread on loaves of bread.

Miss Betty's Biscuits

2 cups self-rising flour
½ cup shortening

⅔ cup milk

Preheat oven to 500 degrees. Place sifted flour in a mixing bowl. Cut in shortening until mixture resembles coarse crumbs or peas. Blend in milk until dough leaves sides of bowl. Knead gently on floured wax paper. Roll dough about ½ inch thick, cut out and place on greased baking sheet. Place about 1 inch apart for crusty biscuits or touching for softer biscuits. Bake 8 to 10 minutes.

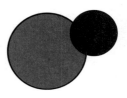

Baked French Toast

1 loaf Texas toast, cut in diagonal
   1 inch slices
8 eggs
2 cups milk
1½ cups half & half

2 teaspoons vanilla extract
¼ teaspoon cinnamon
¾ cup margarine
1⅓ cups brown sugar
3 tablespoons corn syrup

Arrange bread in greased 9x13 inch baking dish. Beat eggs, milk, cream, vanilla, and cinnamon. Pour over bread, cover, refrigerate over night. Combine margarine, sugar and syrup in saucepan until bubbly. Pour over bread and egg mixture. Bake at 350 degrees, uncovered for 40 minutes.

Sausage Cornbread

1 pound sausage
1½ cups self-rising cornmeal
¾ cup milk
2 eggs

2 cups shredded sharp Cheddar
   cheese
1 can cream style corn
¼ cup vegetable oil
   chopped onion (if desired)

In skillet, cook the sausage and onion until meat is browned and onion is tender; drain. In above, combine cornmeal, corn, milk, eggs and oil. Pour half into a greased 10 inch ovenproof skillet. Sprinkle with the sausage mixture and cheese. Spread the remaining cornmeal mixture on the top. Bake at 425 degrees for 45 minutes or until cornbread is golden brown.

Cheesy Cornbread

4	slices bacon	¾	cup mayonnaise
1	(16 ounce) package cornbread mix	1	cup shredded Swiss or Cheddar
2	eggs, beaten		cheese
1	(15 ounce) can cream styled corn		

Cook bacon in an 8 inch cast iron skillet until crisp. Remove bacon, reserving 2 tablespoons drippings. Heat skillet with drippings in a 425 degrees oven for 5 minutes. Combine crumbled bacon, cornbread mix and remaining 4 ingredients, stirring just until dry ingredients are moistened. Remove skillet from oven. Pour mixture into skillet. Bake at 425 degrees for 35 minutes or until golden brown.

Cranberry Walnut Bread

¾	cup butter	1½	teaspoons baking soda
3	cups white sugar	2¼	cups orange juice
3	eggs, beaten	3	tablespoons orange zest
6	cups all-purpose flour	3	cups chopped cranberries
1	tablespoon salt	1½	cups chopped walnuts
1½	tablespoons baking powder		

Preheat oven to 350 degrees. Grease 3 (8x4 inch) loaf pans. Blend together butter, sugar and eggs. Sift together the flour, salt, baking powder and baking soda. Add to wet ingredients, alternating with orange juice. Mix in the orange rind, cranberries and walnuts. Stir until just combined and pour into prepared pans. Bake for 35 minutes or until toothpick inserted in center comes out clean.

Texas–Mexican Cornbread

1	medium onion, chopped	¼	cup oil
1	cup cornmeal	1-1½	jalapeño peppers, chopped finely
¼	cup flour	½-1	cup grated cheese
1	egg, beaten	1	small can cream-style corn

Mix all ingredients except cheese and pour half into oiled, hot medium iron skillet. Spread with grated cheese and pour remaining batter on top of cheese. Bake in preheated oven at 425 degrees until done and firm.

Pumpkin Bread

3	cups sugar	1	teaspoon nutmeg
1	cup salad oil	1	teaspoon allspice
4	eggs	1	teaspoon cinnamon
2	cups cooked pumpkin	½	teaspoon cloves
3½	cups flour	⅔	cup water

Cream sugar and oil together; add eggs and pumpkin, mix well. Sift together dry ingredients and add to mixture with water. This makes two 9x5-inch loaves. Bake at 350 degrees for 1½ hours or until done.

Broccoli Cornbread

1½	sticks margarine	4	eggs
2	boxes Jiffy cornbread mix	1	small onion, finely chopped
8	ounces cottage cheese	1	(10 ounce) box frozen chopped broccoli
4	ounces mozzarella cheese		

Cook broccoli in microwave for 5 to 6 minutes. Melt margarine sticks in 9x13-inch baking dish. Mix all ingredients and pour into dish with melted margarine. Bake at 400 degrees for 30 minutes or until golden brown.

Cocoa Waffles

¼ cup butter or margarine, melted
½ cup cocoa
1 tablespoon oil
¾ cup sugar
2 eggs

1 teaspoon vanilla
½ teaspoon salt
½ teaspoon baking soda
1 cup unsifted all-purpose flour
½ cup buttermilk

Stir together melted butter or margarine, cocoa and oil until smooth. Blend in sugar, eggs and vanilla. Combine flour, baking soda and salt; add alternately with buttermilk to cocoa mixture. Bake in waffle iron according to manufacturer's directions; carefully remove waffle from iron. Serve warm with butter and confectioners sugar, or top with ice cream and chocolate syrup. Makes 8 to 10 waffles.

Mini Chip Pancakes

2 cups buttermilk baking mix
2 eggs
1 cup milk

½ cup semi-sweet chocolate mini chips

Combine buttermilk baking mix, eggs and milk in medium bowl; beat until smooth. Stir in mini chips. Pour 2 tablespoons batter onto hot, lightly greased griddle. Bake until bubbles appear. Turn; bake other side until browned. Serve warm with butter; sprinkle with confectioners sugar, if desired. Makes about 18 pancakes.

Cheddar Bay Biscuits

2 cups Bisquick
⅔ cup milk
½ cup grated Cheddar cheese

¼ cup melted butter
½ teaspoon garlic powder

Mix Bisquick, milk and cheese together for 30 seconds. Drop onto ungreased baking sheets (8 small lumps per sheet). Bake at 450 degrees for 8 to 10 minutes. Mix garlic powder and melted butter; brush on warm biscuits.

Peach Muffins

1½ cups self-rising flour
1   cup sugar
2   eggs, beaten
½   teaspoon vanilla extract

½   cup oil
1¼   cups canned or fresh peaches, chopped

Combine all ingredients together. Spoon into greased muffin tins. Bake at 350 degrees for 25 minutes.

Sausage Muffins

1   pound pork sausage, browned, drained
1   cup all-purpose flour
1   cup self-rising cornmeal

1   (8 ounce) package French onion dip
½   cup milk
⅛   teaspoon salt

Mix all ingredients together. Pour into greased muffin tins. Bake at 375 degrees for 15 minutes.

Marshmallow Roll-Ups

1   (10 ounce) can biscuits
3   tablespoons margarine, softened
¼   cup cinnamon & sugar mixture

30   small marshmallows
½   cup confectioners' sugar
2   tablespoons milk

Roll each biscuit out on floured surface. Spread butter on each biscuit. Sprinkle cinnamon and sugar on both sides. Place 3 marshmallows in center of dough and seal, pinching dough together. Place each biscuit in greased muffin tin, seamed side down. Bake at 350 degrees for 12 minutes. Mix confectioners' sugar and milk until smooth. Spread over cooked biscuits.

Zucchini Bread

2 cups self-rising flour
2 cups sugar
2 eggs
1 cup oil

2 cups grated zucchini
1 teaspoon cinnamon
1 teaspoon vanilla extract
1 cup chopped nuts

Mix all ingredients together. Divide evenly between 2 greased and floured loaf pans. Bake at 350 degrees for about 1 hour. Test to see if done.

Orange Breakfast Ring

2 (10 count) cans biscuits
⅓ cup margarine, melted
1 cup sugar

1 (3 ounce) package cream cheese, softened
½ cup confectioners' sugar
2 tablespoons orange juice

Dip biscuits in margarine, then sugar. Line greased Bundt pan with biscuits. Bake at 350 degrees for 30 minutes. Mix together remaining ingredients. Spread mixture over biscuits after removing from pan.

Apple Dumplings

1 (10 count) can biscuits
6 apples, peeled, chopped
1 (12 ounce) can 7-Up

1 cup sugar
1 stick margarine
1½ teaspoons cinnamon

Roll out each biscuit thinly. Spoon equal amount of chopped apple on each biscuit. Fold up to enclose apples, crimping edges to seal. Place in 9x13 inch dish. Combine remaining ingredients in saucepan. Boil for 2 minutes and pour over dumplings. Bake at 325 degrees for 30 minutes.

NOTES

Taste of Soups & Salads

White Chili

5 (15.8 ounce) cans great Northern
   beans
1 (10 ounce) can chicken
1 (4½ ounce) can chopped green
   chiles
1 small onion, chopped
2 tablespoons ground cumin

2 teaspoons white pepper
2 tablespoons chopped parsley
2 (16 ounce) cans chicken broth
1 (8 ounce) package shredded
   Pepper Jack cheese
   water to cover beans

Mix all ingredients, (except cheese). Add enough water with chicken broth to cover beans. Cover and let simmer about 30 minutes. Add cheese to your liking. Serves 8 to 10.

Original Potato Cheese Soup

6 cups cubed potatoes
4 cups water or to cover
1 chopped onion
½ cup chopped celery or
   ½ teaspoon celery seed

   salt and pepper to taste
8 ounces loaf processed cheese
1 (8 ounce) carton sour cream

Cook all ingredients, except for cheese and sour cream, until potatoes are tender. Add cheese and turn stove down to simmer. When cheese is melted add sour cream and heat through. Do not boil.

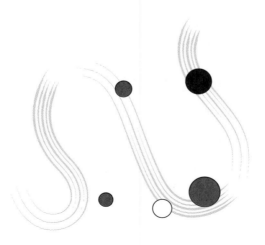

Yummy Potato Soup

3   cans chicken broth
8   medium potatoes, diced
2   cans cream of onion soup
2   cans cream of celery soup

1   (10 ounce) package shredded
    Monterey Jack Cheese with
    peppers
1   pint half & half

Place diced potatoes in chicken broth and allow to cook until potatoes are soft. Add creamed soups and simmer until mixed well. Add shredded cheese and melt in soup mixture. Add half & half and mix until well blended. Makes approximately 1 gallon of soup.

Baked Potato Soup

4   large potatoes
⅔   cup butter
⅔   cup flour
1½   quarts milk
     salt and pepper to taste

4   green onions, chopped
1   cup sour cream
2   cups crumbled crisp cooked bacon
1   (5 ounce) package shredded
     Cheddar cheese

Bake potatoes in 350 degrees oven until tender. Cut potatoes in half and scoop out of skin and set aside. Melt butter in saucepan. Slowly blend in flour. Gradually add milk to the butter-flour mixture, whisking constantly. Whisk in salt and pepper and simmer over low heat, stirring constantly. When milk mixture is very hot, whisk in potatoes and onions. Whisk well, add sour cream and crumbled bacon. Heat thoroughly. Add cheese and serve with crusty French bread.

Louisiana Chicken Gumbo

1 chicken
1 chopped onion
2 stalks celery
1 small bell pepper, chopped
2 cloves garlic, chopped

1 bunch green onions, chopped
2 links chopped, cooked, smoked
   sausage
2 tablespoons Savoie's Roux
   salt and pepper to taste

Boil chicken, cool, de-bone, and chop up. Return to chicken broth along with other ingredients. Season with salt, black and red pepper to taste. Serve over rice.

Corn Chowder

5 slices bacon
1 large onion, chopped
2 cups cubed potatoes, cooked until
   tender
1 (15¼ ounce) can whole kernel corn

1 (14¾ ounce) can cream style corn
1 (10¾ ounce) can cream of
   mushroom soup
2½ cups milk
   salt and pepper to taste

Fry bacon until crisp and set aside. Sauté onions in bacon grease and drain off. Add all other ingredients and bring to a slight boil. Serve with bacon crumbled on top.

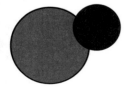

Sante Fe Soup

2 pounds ground beef
1 chopped onion
1 (15 ounce) can black beans
1 (15 ounce) can pinto beans
1 (16 ounce) red kidney beans
2 (11 ounce) cans white shoepeg corn
1 (14½ ounce) can diced tomatoes

1 (10 ounce) can tomatoes and green chiles
2 cups water
2 (1¼ ounce) packages taco seasoning
1 (1 ounce) package dry ranch dressing

Brown meat and onions; drain fat. Add other ingredients, including all juices and simmer for 1 hour.

Potato Broccoli Cheese Soup

1½ quarts water
4 chicken bouillon cubes
2½ cups diced red potatoes
½ package frozen broccoli

3 tablespoons butter
½ cup onions
1 can cream of chicken soup
1 pound Velveeta

Boil water in large pot; add potatoes, bouillon and broccoli. Boil for 10 minutes. While boiling, sauté onions in butter and add to potatoes. Add cream of chicken soup and Velveeta. Stir slowly for about 10 minutes until melted.

Shrimp and Okra Gumbo

1½ pounds de-veined shrimp
1 quart smothered okra
1 tablet Roux
1 cup chopped onions

1 cup chopped bell pepper
2 quarts shrimp stock
salt and pepper to taste

Boil shrimp shells 15 minutes to make a stock in 2 quarts water. Add roux to stock. When roux is dissolved, add cooked okra, onions, bell pepper and cook for 20 minutes. Add shrimp and continue cooking for 30 minutes. Adjust thickness with water as you like it. Pour over hot rice in bowls.

Vegetable Chowder

½	cup chopped green pepper	3	cups water
½	cup chopped onion	3	chicken bouillon cubes
¼	cup butter	1	teaspoon salt
1	cup diced potatoes	¼	teaspoon pepper
1	cup diced celery	½	cup flour
1	cup diced cauliflower	2	cups milk
1	cup diced carrots	1	tablespoon parsley
1	cup diced broccoli	3	cups shredded Cheddar cheese

In soup kettle, sauté green pepper and onion in butter until tender. Add all vegetables, water, bouillon cubes and salt and pepper. Bring to a boil. Reduce heat and simmer 20 minutes. Combine flour and milk until smooth. Stir into pan and bring to a boil again, stirring for 2 minutes. Just before serving add cheese and stir until melted.

Golden Butternut Squash Soup

2	butternut squash, halved and seeded	1	onion, chopped
2	tablespoons butter	2	(16 ounce) can chicken broth
2	cloves garlic, minced	½	teaspoon salt
			cracked black pepper to taste

Preheat oven to 375 degrees. Place squash halves, cut side down, in a large roasting or baking pan. Add water to a depth of ½ inch. Bake for 46 to 60 minutes or until tender when pierced with a knife. Let cool: spoon out flesh, and set aside. Melt butter in a large Dutch oven or soup pot over medium-high heat. Add garlic and onion; cook 3 to 5 minutes or until tender. Stir reserved squash, broth and salt. Bring to a boil, reduce heat, and simmer 15 minutes. Place ⅓ of mixture into container of blender, and blend until puréed. Repeat procedure with remaining squash mixture. Serve immediately or chill. Sprinkle each serving with a small amount of black pepper, if desired. Serves 6.

California Waldorf Salad

1 cup seedless green grapes, halved	1 cup diced cooked chicken breast
1 cup diced apple	½ cup heavy cream
1 cup sliced celery	½ cup mayonnaise
1 cup chopped pecans	1 teaspoon lemon juice
1 cup diced Swiss cheese	1 tablespoon sugar

Toss first 6 ingredients. Whip cream, add remaining ingredients and blend well. Fold dressing into salad and serve cold.

Mixed Vegetable Salad

1 (16 ounce) can English peas	½ cup chopped green onion
1 (16 ounce) can white shoe peg corn, drained	1 cup sugar
	1 teaspoon salt
1 (16 ounce) can French style green beans, drained	½ teaspoon pepper
	½ cup vegetable oil
½ cup diced celery	¾ cup vinegar

Combine vegetables, tossing lightly. Combine remaining ingredients in a medium saucepan; bring to a boil over low heat, stirring occasionally. Pour over vegetables, stirring gently to blend well. Cover and refrigerate 24 hours.

Poppy Seed Dressing

⅓ cup sugar	2 teaspoons onion juice
½ teaspoon dry mustard	½ cup vegetable oil
½ teaspoon salt	2 teaspoons poppy seeds
3 tablespoons white vinegar	

Place sugar, seasonings, vinegar, and onion juice in blender container; cover and blend. Gradually add oil in a slow, steady stream; blend until thickened. Stir in poppy seeds. Makes about 1 cup. Serve over mixed fresh fruit or on green salad.

Fruited Chicken Salad

3 cups cooked chicken, cubed or cut into slices
3 cups cooked brown and wild rice, chilled
1½ cups sliced strawberries
1½ cups orange slices
¾ cup green grapes
½ cup sliced bananas
¼ cup walnuts
2 tablespoons honey
2 tablespoons lemon juice
1 tablespoon orange juice
12 large Romaine lettuce leaves

Combine Chicken, rice, fruit and nuts in large bowl. Combine honey, lemon juice and orange juice in small bowl; toss with chicken mixture. Refrigerate. Serve on lettuce leaves.

Melon Salad

1 cup watermelon, cut into bite-size pieces
1 cup cantaloupe, cut into bite-size pieces
1 cup honeydew, cut into bite-size pieces
1-2 tablespoons powdered sugar
¼ cup lemon or orange juice

Mix ½ melons and sugar together well. Add rest of melons and juice. Sprinkle remaining sugar and mix well. Refrigerate.

Cornbread Salad

1 pan cornbread, cooled
6-8 green onions (chopped with green part)
6-8 radishes, sliced or chopped (optional)
½ green pepper, chopped
2 peeled tomatoes, chopped
¼ cup mayonnaise
¼ cup cucumber ranch dressing
1-2 teaspoons mustard
salt and pepper to taste

Crumble cooled cornbread in large bowl. Add vegetables. Combine mayonnaise, dressing and mustard. Toss lightly into cornbread mixture.

Picnic Potato Salad

3   pounds potatoes
⅓   cup bottled French dressing
3   tablespoons vinegar
1   teaspoon salt
1   (3 ounce) package cream cheese

2   tablespoons grated onion
½   cup mayonnaise or salad dressing
3   hard boiled eggs, sliced
   paprika

Boil potatoes in boiling salted water until tender. Drain. Cool, peel and slice. Place potato slices in a large bowl. Add French dressing, vinegar and salt. Toss lightly. Cover and refrigerate for 45 minutes. Combine cream cheese, onion and mayonnaise or salad dressing. Beat until creamy and smooth. Add to potato mixture. Add 2 sliced eggs. Mix thoroughly. Cover and refrigerate for several hours. To serve, garnish with remaining sliced egg and sprinkle with paprika.

Congealed Strawberry Salad

2   packages strawberry Jell-O
2   cups boiling water
1   (10 ounce) package frozen
    strawberries
1   small can crushed pineapple

1   (8 ounce) package cream cheese
½   cup sugar
1   teaspoon vanilla
1   package Cool Whip
   chopped nuts

Dissolve Jell-O in boiling water. Set aside ¼ cup. Mix remaining Jell-O mixture, frozen strawberries and crushed pineapple; pour in oblong dish or mold and refrigerate until set. Combine Cool Whip with ¼ cup reserved Jell-O mixture. Add cream cheese, sugar and vanilla. Pour over congealed mixture and top with chopped nuts.

Spinach Strawberry Salad

Spinach leaves
green leaf lettuce
mushrooms, sliced

strawberries, sliced
walnuts, chopped

DRESSING

½ cup sugar
2 tablespoons sesame seeds
1 tablespoon poppy seeds
1½ teaspoons minced onion

¼ teaspoon Worcestershire sauce
½ cup vegetable oil
¼ cup apple cider vinegar

Mix salad ingredients. Mix dressing ingredients. Pour dressing over salad and serve.

Congealed Salad

1 small package gelatin, any flavor
1 small can crushed pineapple with juice

1½ cups buttermilk
1 (8 ounce) container Cool Whip

Heat pineapple and gelatin until dissolved. Let cool. Stir in buttermilk. Fold in Cool Whip. Cover and refrigerate.

Although we prefer smooth and creamy,
a little crunchy is in order
to yank us back to the
path that God has chosen for us.

Cranberry Pineapple Salad

1	(20 ounce) can crushed pineapple, in juice	1	(16 ounce) whole berry cranberry sauce
2	(3 ounce) package Jell-O sugar free raspberry flavor gelatin	⅔	cup chopped walnut pieces
		1	apple, chopped

Drain pineapple, reserving juice. Add enough water to juice to measure 2½ cups; pour into saucepan. Bring to boil. Pour over gelatin mixes in large bowl; stir 2 minutes until completely dissolved. Stir in pineapple, cranberry sauce, walnuts and apple. Pour into 2 quart serving dish or can be spooned into 24 paper lined muffin cups. Refrigerate 2 to 3 hours. Serves 24.

Debbie's Chicken Salad

4	cups chicken, cooked and cubed	1	teaspoon salt
1	cup celery, chopped	¼	teaspoon pepper
1	cup seedless grapes, halved	¾	cup mayonnaise
1	package pecan pieces	¼	cup sour cream

Mix all ingredients in order. Chill well and serve on lettuce leaves. Serves 4.

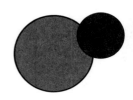

Cole Slaw

1	head cabbage, finely chopped	¼	cup milk
¼	cup shredded carrots	½	cup mayonnaise
⅓	cup sugar	¼	cup buttermilk
½	teaspoon salt	1½	tablespoons white vinegar
⅛	teaspoon pepper	2½	tablespoons lemon juice

Chop cabbage and carrots very fine. Combine sugar, salt, pepper, milk, mayonnaise, buttermilk, vinegar and lemon juice; beat until smooth. Add cabbage and carrots to mixture. Cover and refrigerate at least 2 hours before serving. This is critical for flavor enhancement.

Broccoli Salad

1	large head of broccoli, remove flowers and most tender stems	3	stalks celery, sliced
½	cup raisins	1	can water chestnuts, drained and sliced
6	green onions, sliced		

Combine above ingredients.

DRESSING

1	tablespoon vinegar	1	cup mayonnaise
2	tablespoons sugar		

Mix well and add to salad ingredients. Toss and serve.

Cranberry Salad

2	small boxes strawberry gelatin	1	pound cranberries
2	cups boiling water	⅔	cup sugar
2	apples	½	cup chopped celery, optional
3	oranges	½	cup chopped pecans, optional

Dissolve gelatin in boiling water. Refrigerate to chill. Grind apples and oranges then add the sugar to them. When gelatin begins to set, fold fruit mixture in it. Add celery and pecans at this time if you use them. Cover and refrigerate.

Seven Layer Salad

1	head of lettuce, torn in bite size pieces	1	pint mayonnaise
1	cup celery, chopped	1	(8 ounce) package shredded Cheddar cheese
1	cup onion, chopped	1	(3 ounce) can grated Parmesan cheese
1	cup bell pepper, chopped		
1	large can English peas, drained	1	jar bacon bits

In a large glass bowl, layer ingredients in order given. Cover and refrigerate. Best if made day before serving.

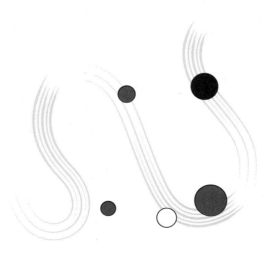

Green Bean, Grape and Pasta Toss

1	(8 ounce) package penne pasta	⅓	cup red vinegar
1	cup pecans	1	teaspoon salt
8	bacon strips	2	cups seedless grapes cut in half
1	pound green beans	⅓	cup diced red onions
1	cup mayonnaise		

Toast pecans. Cover beans in boiling water then put in ice water to stop cooking. Cook pasta. Whisk mayonnaise, red vinegar and salt in a large bowl. Mix with beans, bacon, pasta, grapes and onion.

Curried Chicken Salad

4	cups diced cooked chicken breasts	1	(8 ounce) can crushed pineapple, drained
¾	cup mayonnaise		
1	teaspoon curry powder	1	large apple, finely chopped
½	cup finely chopped celery	½	cup golden raisins
¼	cup finely chopped onion		

Mix mayonnaise and curry powder together. Mix all ingredients together and keep refrigerated.

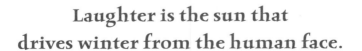

Laughter is the sun that
drives winter from the human face.

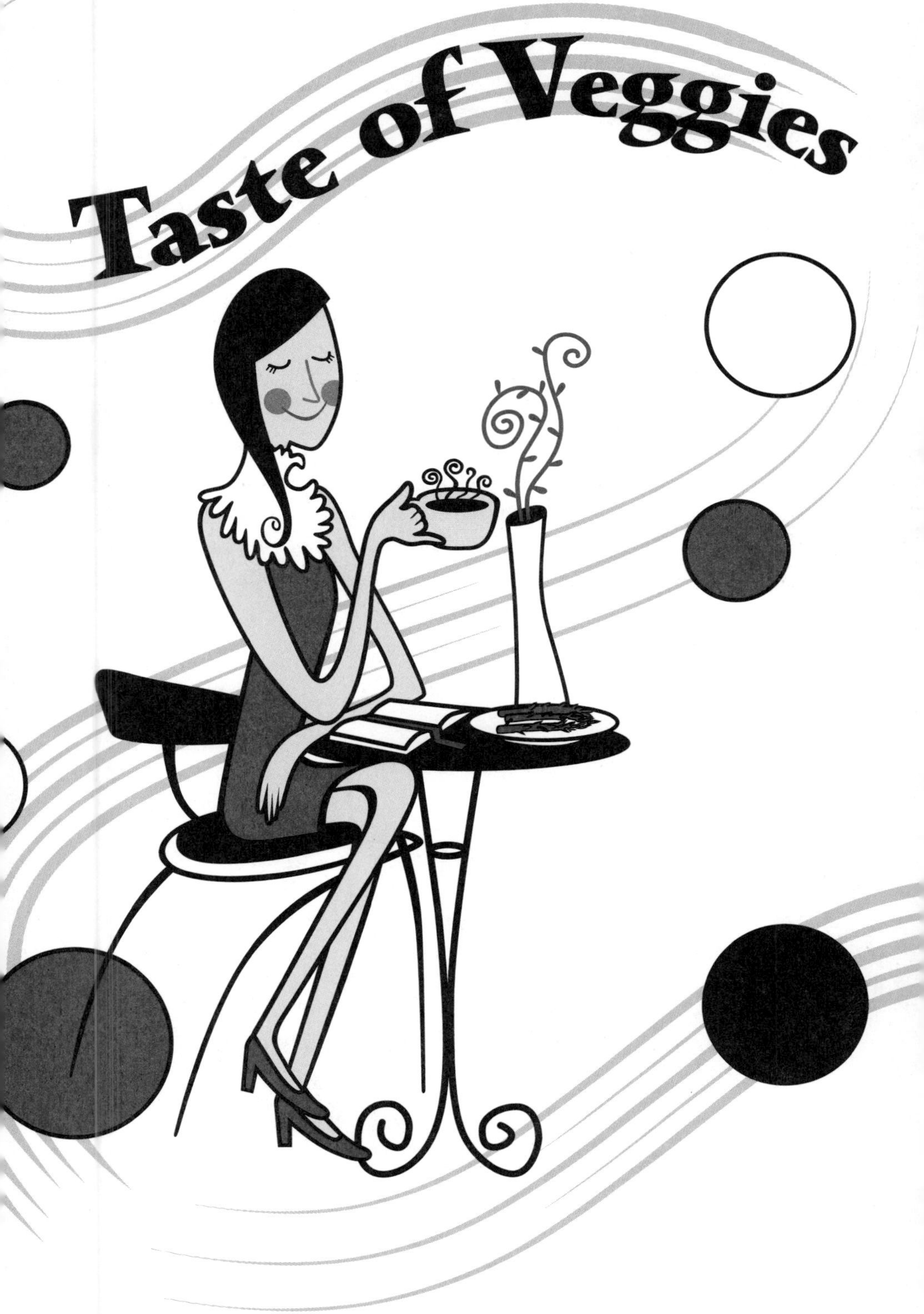
Taste of Veggies

Loaded Mashed Potatoes

4   Russet baking potatoes, peeled
    and cut into chunks
1½ pounds red potatoes, scrubbed
    clean and cut into chunks
1½ teaspoons salt
¼   cup butter or margarine
4   cloves chopped garlic

½   cup heavy cream
¼   cup sour cream
1   cup shredded Cheddar cheese
8   slices bacon, cooked crisp and
    crumbled
¼   cup chopped chives
    pepper to taste

Place potatoes in a large pot and cover with cold water; add salt. Bring to a boil. Reduce heat to a simmer and cook until potatoes are fork-tender about 12 to 15 minutes. Drain completely in a colander. Return potatoes to the cooking pot and place back over low heat. While potatoes cook, melt butter in a small saucepan; add garlic and cook over low heat just until garlic softens. Add cream to the garlic butter and heat through. Remove cream mixture from heat and stir in sour cream. When potatoes are cooked and dry, add butter/sour cream mixture to the pot while mashing with a potato masher to blend all the ingredients and achieve a light texture, being careful not to over mix. Taste and adjust the seasonings with salt and pepper. Just before serving stir in cheese and bacon. Spoon into a serving dish and top with chives.

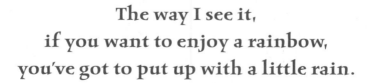

The way I see it,
if you want to enjoy a rainbow,
you've got to put up with a little rain.

Garlic Mashed Potatoes

4	pounds potatoes, peeled	1	(14 ounce) can low-sodium chicken broth
2	teaspoons salt	⅓	cup cream
1	small chopped onion		salt and pepper to taste
6	crushed garlic cloves		
4	tablespoons melted butter or margarine		

Place potatoes in a large pot and cover with cold water; add salt and onion. Bring to a boil. Reduce heat to a simmer and cook until potatoes are tender about 15 to 20 minutes. Drain completely in a colander. Return potatoes to the cooking pot and place back over low heat. Mash potatoes. Melt butter in a small saucepan; add garlic and cook over low heat just until garlic softens. Mash into a paste with butter. Set aside. While potatoes are cooking, bring chicken broth to a boil. Lower heat and simmer until broth is reduced to ¼ cup. Add butter/garlic and milk; heat until hot. Stir milk mixture into potatoes. If potatoes are too stiff, add hot cream, 1 tablespoon at a time until desired consistency is reached.

Potato Bake

2	pounds frozen hash browns	1	stick butter, melted
1	can cream of chicken soup	2	cups crushed cornflakes
1	pint sour cream	1	small onion
¼	pound margarine		

Heat oven to 350 degrees. Spread frozen potatoes in 9x13 inch baking dish. Cut margarine in chunks and put on top of potatoes. Mix soup and sour cream and spread over potatoes and butter. Spread onions and cheese over mixture. Mix stick of melted butter with cornflakes. Spread over top of cheese. Bake 45 minutes.

Sweet Potato Casserole

3 cups sweet potatoes, creamed
2 eggs, beaten
½ cup butter

1 cup sugar
⅓ cup milk
1 teaspoon vanilla extract

TOPPING

1 cup brown sugar
½ cup flour

⅓ cup butter
1 cup chopped pecans

Mix together all ingredients for casserole and pour into dish. Mix together ingredients for topping and sprinkle over casserole. Bake at 350 degrees for 25 minutes.

Sweet Potato Medallions

2 tablespoons butter or margarine
3 large sweet potatoes, peeled and
   sliced ½ inch thick

1 cup apple juice or cider
½ teaspoon cinnamon
1 tablespoon sugar

Melt butter in a large skillet. Fry potatoes in butter 1 minute on each side. Pour apple juice into skillet; sprinkle potatoes with cinnamon and sugar. Cover tightly. Cook until almost all the juice is absorbed and potatoes are tender. Uncover and continue cooking until juice is reduced to a syrupy glaze. Remove from heat and spoon glaze over potatoes. Serve hot.

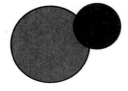

Asparagus Casserole

1   roll crushed Ritz crackers
1   can green asparagus spears
1   can English peas
½   cup chopped onion
1   can sliced water chestnuts

1   can chicken soup with 1 can water, mixed
2   cups grated sharp cheese
½   stick margarine, melted

Layer in order half the crackers, half the asparagus, half the peas, half the onions, half the water chestnuts, half the soup and water mixture and half the cheese. Repeat. Pour the melted margarine over the top. Bake at 350 degrees for 40 minutes.

Pinto Bean Casserole

2   cans pinto beans
1   can Ro-Tel tomatoes, diced
½   cup mushrooms

1   pound ground beef
1   small chopped onion
1   package cornbread mix, prepared

Cook and drain meat and onions. Add other ingredients. Pour in casserole dish. Pour prepared cornbread mix over top of bean mixture and bake 30 minutes at 350 degrees.

Squash Casserole

4   cups squash
1   cup mayonnaise
2   eggs, beaten
1   can mushroom soup

1   can celery soup
1   cup chopped celery
1   small onion
18   Ritz crackers

Combine all ingredients in baking dish, top with crushed crackers. Bake 45 minutes at 375 degrees.

Onion Roasted Potatoes

1   envelope onion soup mix   2   pounds chunked potatoes
2   cups vegetable oil

Preheat oven to 450 degrees. Place all ingredients in large plastic bag. Shake until potatoes are evenly coated. Empty potatoes in baking dish and bake 40 minutes or until potatoes are tender and brown. Stir occasionally.

Marinated Carrots

2   pounds carrots, peeled and sliced   ¾   cup vinegar
1   medium onion   1   teaspoon mustard
1   bell pepper   1   teaspoon salt
1   can tomato soup   1   teaspoon Worcestershire sauce
½   cup oil   pepper to taste
1   cup sugar

Cook carrots until tender; drain and cool. Slice onion and bell pepper. Mix with carrots. Mix together and bring to boil the soup, oil, sugar, vinegar, mustard, Worcestershire, salt and pepper. Pour over carrot mixture and let stand 24 hours.

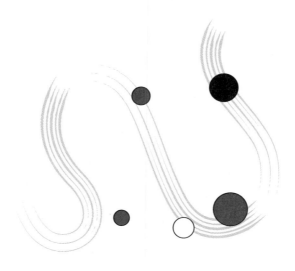

Spinach Cheese Pie

1   (9 inch) pie crust
1   (10 ounce) package frozen
      chopped spinach, thawed and
      drained
1   cup shredded Swiss cheese
      egg substitute equal to 4 eggs
⅓   cup green onion, sliced
4   eggs, slightly beaten
¼   teaspoon Worcestershire sauce
¼   cup grated Parmesan cheese
¾   cup half & half or evaporated milk
½   teaspoon salt

Prick crust and bake at 450 degrees for 8 minutes. Cool. Layer ½ spinach, ½ cheese and ½ onion, then repeat. Combine other ingredients and pour over layers. Bake 10 minutes at 450 degrees and then 25 minutes at 350 degrees. Cool 5 minutes before slicing.

Spinach Casserole

2   packages frozen spinach, chopped
2   (8 ounce) packages cream cheese,
      softened
¼   pound butter or margarine,
      softened
¼   teaspoon salt
1½ cups grated Parmesan cheese

Preheat oven to 350 degrees. Cook spinach until just done. Drain well. Mix spinach with cream cheese, butter and salt. Put into casserole and cover with Parmesan cheese. Bake for 30 minutes or until cheese melts.

Corn Casserole

4   tablespoons flour
3   tablespoons margarine, softened
1   cup milk
1   can cream of chicken soup
3   (15 ounce) cans whole corn,
      drained
½   teaspoon salt
½   teaspoon pepper
1   stick margarine, melted
36   Ritz crackers, crushed

Mix first 3 ingredients together. Add next 4 ingredients and cook until thickened. Pour into greased 2 quart casserole dish. Mix the stick of margarine and crackers. Spread on top of mixture and bake at 350 degrees for 30 minutes.

Sunday Green Beans Casserole

1   large chopped onion
¼   cup margarine or butter
1   can golden mushroom soup
⅛   teaspoon Tabasco sauce
1   cup medium grated Cheddar
      cheese
      salt and pepper to taste

2   (16 ounce) cans whole or French
      style green beans, drained
2   (5 ounce) cans water chestnuts,
      sliced
½   cup slivered almonds
1   can French fried onion rings
6   slices bacon, sautéed and
      crumbled

Sauté onion in margarine. Add soup, Tabasco, cheese, salt and pepper; heat until cheese melts. Add crumbled bacon to sauce. In 8x8 inch casserole dish layer half beans, sliced chestnuts, almonds and sauce. Repeat layers with remaining half of ingredients. Top with onion rings. Bake at 350 degrees for 45 minutes.

Bacon Wrapped Green Beans

1   package regular cut bacon

3   cans whole green beans

Preheat oven to 400 degrees, after opening the package of bacon, cut in half down the middle. Drain and empty the cans of green beans in a bowl. Take about 4 to 8 whole green beans depending on the size of bundle you desire and wrap them in a half piece of bacon. If the beans are thin use 8, if the beans are thick use 4. After wrapping a green bean bundle, place it seam down in an 8½x11 inch dish. After the dish is full, cook until bacon is done. Cover with foil and cook for 30 minutes and then remove foil and continue to cook. Remove from oven once the bacon is cooked; it will not be crispy.

Veg-All Casserole

2 (15 ounce) cans Veg-All, drained
1 cup mayonnaise
1 cup chopped celery
1 cup chopped onion
1 cup shredded Cheddar cheese
1½ cups crushed Ritz crackers
4 tablespoons melted butter

Combine first 5 ingredients and put in 2 quart casserole dish. Melt 4 tablespoons of butter and mix with Ritz crackers. Sprinkle on top of mixture. Bake for 20 minutes at 350 degrees.

Baked Corn

2 (3 ounce) packages cream cheese
¼ cup milk
¼ cup butter
garlic salt to taste
salt and pepper to taste
2 jalapeño peppers, chopped
2 (16 ounce) cans shoe peg corn, drained

Combine cream cheese, milk, butter and cook slowly, stirring constantly. Add garlic salt, salt, pepper and jalapeños. Add corn and put in greased dish. Bake uncovered at 350 degrees for 30 minutes.

Caribbean Black Beans

3 strips bacon
½ cup diced onion
½ cup red bell pepper
2 tablespoon minced garlic
1 (30 ounce) can black beans, rinsed and drained
½ cup chicken broth
1 (15 ounce) can diced tomatoes

Sauté bacon in large pan over medium heat for 5 minutes. Remove from pan. Add onion and pepper. Sauté for 3 minutes. Stir in garlic, sauté for 1 minute. Strain bacon, beans, tomatoes and broth. Bring to boil. Reduce and simmer for 20 minutes. Season with salt and pepper.

Baked Potato Wedges

3-4 medium baking potatoes
3 tablespoons melted margarine

seasoned salt

Scrub potatoes. Do not peel. Cut each potato lengthwise in quarters. Dip each potato wedge in melted margarine, covering each side; arrange skin side down on a shallow baking pan. Sprinkle with seasoned salt. Bake, uncovered, at 400 degrees for about 1 hour or until golden brown and tender when pierced.

Meaty Baked Beans

½ pound hot bulk sausage, cooked
  and drained
½ pound bacon, cooked (reserve
  3 tablespoons drippings)
1 large onion, chopped
1 medium bell pepper, chopped
1 teaspoon garlic powder
3 pound can pork & beans

2 tablespoons Worcestershire sauce
1 teaspoon liquid smoke
¼ teaspoon black pepper
2 tablespoons prepared mustard
1 teaspoon dry mustard
¼ cup molasses
1 (6 ounce) can tomato paste

Sauté onion and bell pepper in bacon drippings. Combine with all other ingredients and pour into 9x13 inch baking dish. Bake, covered, for 45 minutes at 350 degrees. Remove cover, and continue baking for another 30 minutes.

Elegant Potatoes

8-10 medium potatoes, peeled,
  quartered
1 (8 ounce) package cream cheese,
  softened
1 (8 ounce) package sour cream

¼ cup butter
⅓ cup chopped chives
  salt and pepper, to taste
  paprika

Boil potatoes until tender. Using electric mixer, beat sour cream and cream cheese together. Add hot potatoes and beat until smooth. Add butter, chives, salt, and pepper. Pour into a well greased baking dish, dot with additional butter and sprinkle paprika over top. Bake 350 degrees for 25 minutes. Makes 8 to 10 servings. (Can be prepared ahead and refrigerated.)

Stuffed Zucchini

6-8 medium zucchini
1 cup bulk sausage, cooked and drained
¼ cup margarine
½ cup diced onion

½ cup diced green pepper
½ cup bread crumbs
2 eggs, beaten
1 cup mild Cheddar cheese

Cut zucchini in half, remove seeds. Cover with water in a saucepan and bring to a boil. Turn off heat and let stand 3 minutes; drain. Sauté onion and green pepper in margarine. Combine sausage, onion, pepper, bread, and eggs. Fill zucchini and sprinkle with cheese. Bake at 350 degrees for 25 to 30 minutes or until knife inserted in stuffing comes out clean.

Baked Risotto with Asparagus, Spinach and Parmesan

1 tablespoon olive oil
1 cup finely chopped onion
1 cup Arborio (risotto) rice
8 cups spinach leaves, torn into pieces
2 cups chicken broth

¼ teaspoon salt
¼ teaspoon ground nutmeg
½ cup grated Parmesan cheese, divided
1½ cups diagonally sliced asparagus

Preheat oven to 400 degrees. Lightly coat 13x9-inch baking dish with nonstick cooking spray. Heat olive oil in large skillet over medium-high heat. Add onion; cook and stir 4 minutes or until tender. Add rice; stir to coat with oil. Stir in spinach, a handful at a time, adding more as it wilts. Add broth, salt and nutmeg. Reduce heat and simmer 7 minutes. Stir in ¼ cup cheese. Transfer to prepared baking dish. Cover tightly and bake 15 minutes. Remove from oven and stir in asparagus; sprinkle with remaining ¼ cup cheese. Cover and bake 15 minutes more or until liquid is absorbed.

Saucy Broccoli Spaghetti

3 ounces uncooked spaghetti
1 (10 ounce) package frozen chopped broccoli
½ cup thinly sliced leek, white part only
½ cup skim milk
2 teaspoons cornstarch
2 teaspoons chopped fresh oregano or ½ teaspoon dried oregano
⅛ teaspoon hot pepper sauce
3 tablespoons cream cheese, softened
1 tablespoon grated Romano or Parmesan cheese
1 tablespoon chopped fresh parsley

Prepare spaghetti according to package directions, omitting salt; drain and keep warm. Meanwhile cook broccoli and leek together according to package directions for broccoli, omitting salt. Drain; reserve ¼ cup liquid. Add additional water, if needed, to make ¼ cup. Combine milk, cornstarch, oregano and pepper sauce in medium saucepan. Stir in reserved ¼ cup liquid. Cook and stir over medium heat until mixture boils and thickens. Stir in cream cheese. Cook and stir until cheese melts. Stir in vegetables; heat through. Serve vegetable mixture over pasta. Sprinkle with Romano cheese and parsley.

Heavenly Potatoes

1 (24 ounce) package frozen hashbrown potatoes
1¾ cups grated sharp Cheddar cheese
1 can cream of chicken soup
1 (8 ounce) package sour cream
1 stick (or less) melted butter
1 teaspoon salt
1 medium onion

Mix all ingredients together. (Works better if potatoes are defrosted.) Pour into baking dish. May be wrapped in foil for freezer or baked. Bake at 350 degrees for 45 minutes to 1 hour.

French Fried Okra

1	pound fresh okra	2	cups self-rising flour
½	teaspoon salt		vegetable oil
1	cup buttermilk		

Wash okra and drain well. Remove tips and stems; cut okra into ½" slices. Sprinkle okra slices with salt; add buttermilk, stirring until well coated. Let stand 15 minutes, then drain okra well. Coat okra in flour. Deep fry in hot oil until golden brown. Drain on paper towels.

Green Bean and Corn Casserole

1	(15 ounce) can French-style green beans, drained	1	(10¾ ounce) can cream of celery soup
1	(15 ounce) can white shoe peg corn, drained		grated Cheddar cheese
1	(8 ounce) package sour cream		Ritz crackers, crushed
			sliced almonds
		1	stick butter, melted

Preheat oven to 350 degrees. Place beans and corn in a greased 2 quart casserole dish. In small mixing bowl, combine sour cream and soup. Mix thoroughly. Pour mixture over vegetables. Cover the top of casserole with cheese. Cover cheese with crackers. Sprinkle almonds on top and pour butter over casserole. Bake for 30 minutes or until bubbly. Makes 6 to 8 servings.

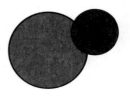

Broccoli-Rice Casserole

CASSEROLE

2	(10 ounce) packages frozen chopped broccoli, thawed and drained	1	can cream of chicken soup, undiluted
½	cup diced onions	1	(8 ounce) jar Cheese Whiz
½	cup butter or margarine, melted	½	cup milk
		2	cups cooked rice

TOPPING

1	stick butter or margarine, melted	1	sleeve Ritz crackers, crushed

Sauté broccoli and onions in ½ cup melted butter. Add soup, Cheese Whiz, and milk. Cook until cheese melts and is blended. Remove from heat and add cooked rice. Put in casserole dish. Mix crushed crackers with melted butter and spread on top of casserole. Bake at 350 degrees for 45 minutes.

Creamed New Potatoes

2½	pounds unpeeled small red potatoes, cut into 1 inch slices	1	bunch green onions, chopped
1	teaspoon salt	1	teaspoon dried thyme
1	(8 ounce) package cream cheese, cubed	1	teaspoon dried tarragon
1	cup buttermilk	¼	teaspoon pepper
		3	tablespoons minced fresh parsley

Place potatoes in a large saucepan and cover with water; add salt. Bring to a boil. Reduce heat; cover and cook for 15 to 20 minutes or until tender. Meanwhile, in another saucepan, combine the cream cheese and buttermilk; cook and stir over medium heat until cheese is melted and mixture is smooth. Remove from the heat; add the onions, thyme, tarragon and pepper. Drain potatoes and place in a serving bowl; add cream sauce and toss to coat. Sprinkle with parsley. Serves 6.

Roasted Plum Tomatoes

8 plum tomatoes
1 tablespoon olive oil
¼ teaspoon dried thyme

½ teaspoon coarse salt
¼ teaspoon ground pepper

Preheat oven to 425 degrees. Core tomatoes; halve each lengthwise. Transfer to a rimmed baking sheet; toss with olive oil, dried thyme, coarse salt, and ground pepper until coated. Arrange in a single layer, cut sides up. Bake until soft, about 30 minutes.

Fried Green Tomatoes

4 green tomatoes
salt to taste
pepper to taste

1½ cups flour
shortening

Slice tomatoes into ¼ inch slices. Sprinkle with salt and pepper. Coat in flour. Brown in hot shortening until crisp. Absorb excess oil by placing on paper towels. Serve hot.

Stuffed Bell Pepper

12 medium bell peppers
1 pound ground meat
1 chopped onion
3 tablespoons catsup

salt and pepper to taste
20 Ritz cracker crumbs
2 cups cooked rice

Prepare peppers by cutting off tops and taking out seeds. Keep the bits of peppers to grind. Sauté ground meat and onions. Add the ground peppers and seasonings. Add catsup. Cook down about 30 minutes. Mix with cooked rice. Stuff pepper cups. Bake in large pan at 350 degrees for 30 minutes. Add a little water in bottom of pan to keep from sticking. Add crumbs on top.

Roasted Vegetables

10	tiny red new potatoes	1	teaspoon pepper
10	baby carrots	½	teaspoon lemon pepper
1	small white onion, cut into wedges	1	medium red bell pepper, seeded
¼	cup olive oil		and cut into ½ inch strips
4	cloves garlic, minced	3	yellow squash, sliced
3	tablespoons fresh lemon juice	3	zucchini, sliced
2	tablespoons chopped fresh	15	whole fresh button or creamy
	oregano or rosemary		mushrooms
1	teaspoon salt		

Preheat oven to 450 degrees. Place potatoes, carrots and onions in a 9x13 inch baking dish. Mix olive oil, garlic, lemon juice, oregano/rosemary, salt, pepper, and lemon pepper in a small bowl. Drizzle over vegetables and toss. Roast uncovered 20 to 30 minutes. Stir in bell pepper, squash, zucchini and mushrooms. Roast an additional 10 to 15 minutes.

Baked Squash Casserole

2	pounds squash	3	tablespoons chopped onion
3	eggs, beaten	½	teaspoon Tabasco sauce
2	teaspoons parsley flakes	2	cups cracker crumbs
½	cup butter or margarine		

Slice squash into ½ inch pieces. Boil 3 minutes or until tender; drain. Add onion, eggs and seasonings. Mix until well blended. Pour into 1 quart buttered casserole dish. Mix butter and crumbs together. Sprinkle over squash. Bake at 350 degrees for 40 minutes, until browned.

Bean Bake

1	(15.8 ounce) can great Northern beans, undrained	1½	tablespoons brown sugar
¼	teaspoon salt	⅓	cup tomato juice
¼	teaspoon prepared mustard	2	tablespoons chopped onion

Combine all ingredients. Bake in small greased casserole dish 30 to 40 minutes at 400 degrees.

Taste of Meats

Skillet Beef Dinner

2   cups rice
1   pound ground chuck
1   can tomato sauce
1   onion, chopped
1   (8 ounce) package cream cheese

salt to taste
pepper to taste
garlic to taste
1   green pepper (optional)
olive oil

Boil rice. Brown meat, add salt and pepper. Pour tomato sauce over meat. Slice onion and sauté in olive oil until clear, turn on low and melt cream cheese over onions. Serve meat over rice and cover with cheese and onion sauce.

Slow Cooker Pot Roast

1   can cream of mushroom soup
1   (2 ounce) package dry onion soup mix
6   small red potatoes, halved

6   medium carrots, cut into 2 inch pieces
3   pound boneless beef bottom round roast or chuck pot roast

Stir soup, onion soup mix, potatoes and carrots in 4 to 5 quart slow cooker. Add beef and turn to coat. Cover and cook on low 8 to 9 hours or until beef is fork tender, or on high 4 to 5 hours.

Mexican Bake

¾	pound extra lean ground beef	1	(10 ounce) package frozen corn
1	onion, chopped	3	(8 inch) whole wheat tortillas
1	green pepper, chopped	½	cup sour cream
2	teaspoons chili powder	¾	cup shredded sharp Cheddar
1¼	cups thick 'n chunky salsa		cheese, divided

Heat oven to 375 degrees. Brown meat with onions and peppers in large skillet on medium-high heat. Stir in chili powder; cook 1 minute. Add salsa and corn; mix well. Simmer 5 minutes. Spread 1 cup meat sauce onto bottom of 8 or 9 inch square baking dish; top with layers of 1 tortilla, ½ cup meat sauce, sour cream and ¼ cup cheese. Cover with 1 tortilla, 1 cup of remaining meat sauce and ¼ cup of remaining cheese; top with remaining tortilla and meat sauce. Cover with foil. Bake 25 minutes or until casserole is heated through. Top with remaining cheese; bake, uncovered, 5 minutes or until melted.

Tater-Topped Casserole

1	pound ground beef	1	cup frozen mixed vegetables
1	small onion, finely chopped	1	cup shredded Cheddar cheese
1	(10¾ ounce) can condensed cream	1	pound frozen bite-size seasoned
	of mushroom soup		potato nuggets
¼	cup milk		

Heat oven to 375 degrees. Brown meat with onions in skillet, stirring occasionally; drain. Spoon into 8 inch square baking dish. Mix soup and milk; pour over meat mixture. Top with layers of mixed vegetables, cheese and potatoes. Bake 45 minutes or until potatoes are golden brown and casserole is heated through.

Quick Chicken Cacciatore

4 boneless and skinless chicken breast pieces
2 medium zucchini, peeled and sliced
1 small onion, cut into large pieces
1 cup fresh mushrooms, cleaned and sliced
3 tablespoons olive oil, divided
1 teaspoon salt
½ teaspoon black pepper
½ teaspoon granulated garlic powder
1 teaspoon oregano
2 teaspoons basil
¼ teaspoon fennel seed, crushed
1 tablespoon water
1 (14 ounce) can petite diced tomatoes
1 (8 ounce) can tomato sauce

Preheat oven to 375 degrees. In a small bowl, mix together the salt, spices and water and set aside. Wash chicken, pat dry. Heat a large skillet over medium-high heat. Add 1 tablespoon of the olive oil. When hot, add chicken breasts. Cook 2 to 3 minutes per side until nicely browned. Remove to a plate. Adding the remaining 1 to 2 tablespoons of oil as needed, quickly brown the zucchini slices, onion, then mushrooms. Keep the pan good and hot; the object is to brown the chicken and veggies without cooking them all the way through. Mix together the spice mix, diced tomatoes and tomato sauce. Pour half of the tomato mixture into a 9x13 inch glass pan. Add the vegetables to the pan. Place the chicken over the vegetables. Pour the remaining tomato mixture over the top of the chicken. Cover the pan and bake until the vegetables are tender and the chicken is cooked through, about 30 to 40 minutes.

Sour Cream Chicken Bake

1 teaspoon garlic salt
1 teaspoon celery seed
1 teaspoon grated lemon rind
1 (8 ounce) container sour cream
8 chicken breasts
1 cup melted butter
1 cup dry breadcrumbs
1 (4 ounce) jar mushroom pieces
¼ cup lemon juice

Preheat oven to 350 degrees. Add garlic salt, celery seed and lemon rind to sour cream and stir. Dip chicken into melted butter, then into sour cream mixture. Roll in breadcrumbs to coat well. Place in buttered casserole. Spread mushrooms evenly over top. Sprinkle with lemon juice and remaining butter. Cover tightly with aluminum foil. Bake for 1 hour. Remove foil and continue baking until lightly browned.

Sour Cream Chicken Enchiladas

2	tablespoons butter or margarine		½	teaspoon coriander
1	medium onion, chopped		¾	teaspoon salt
½	cup chopped green bell pepper		2½	cups chicken broth
2	cups cooked and chopped chicken		1	(8 ounce) container sour cream
1	(4 ounce) can chopped green chilies		1½	cups shredded Monterey Jack cheese, divided
3	tablespoons butter or margarine		12	(6 inch) flour tortillas
¼	cup all-purpose flour			salsa for garnish

Preheat oven to 350 degrees. Melt 2 tablespoons butter in a large skillet. Sauté onion and bell pepper, until limp. Remove from skillet and combine with chicken. Add green chilies. Set aside. In the same skillet, melt 3 tablespoons butter; blend in flour, coriander and salt. Cook over medium-high heat 1 minute, stirring constantly. Slowly stir in chicken broth; bring to a boil and cook until thick and bubbly, stirring constantly. Remove from heat and stir in sour cream and ¾ cup cheese. Stir 1 cup of the sauce into the chicken mixture. Dip a tortilla into remaining sauce. Spoon ¼ cup chicken mixture on the top one third of the tortilla. Fold top of tortilla over filling; fold in sides and continue rolling tortilla to totally encase filling. Place seam side down in a lightly greased 9x13 inch baking dish. Repeat with remaining tortillas and filling. Pour any remaining sauce over tortillas. Cover pan with aluminum foil and bake 20 minutes. Remove foil, sprinkle with remaining cheese and return to oven for 5 additional minutes or until cheese is melted.

There's a time and a place
for screaming, but prayer
needs no special time or place.

Fluffy Rice and Chicken

1	can mushroom soup	1	(4 ounce) can mushroom stems and pieces
1	soup can of milk	1	envelope onion soup mix
¾	cup uncooked rice	4	chicken breast halves

Heat oven to 350 degrees. Mix mushroom soup and milk; reserve ½ cup of the mixture. Mix remaining soup mixture, the rice, mushrooms with liquid and half of the onion soup mix. Pour into ungreased baking dish. Place chicken breasts on top. Pour reserved soup mixture over chicken breasts; sprinkle with remaining onion soup mix. Cover with aluminum foil; bake 1 hour. Uncover; bake 15 minutes longer.

Chicken Fajita Dinner

1½	cups instant white rice, uncooked	1	each: green and red pepper, cut into strips
1½	cups hot water	½	cup thick 'n chunky salsa
1	tablespoon taco seasoning mix	½	cup shredded Cheddar cheese
4	small boneless, skinless chicken breast halves		

Heat oven to 400 degrees. Fold up all sides of each of four 18x12 inch sheets of heavy-duty foil to form 1-inch rim; spray foil with cooking spray. Combine rice, water and taco seasoning; spoon onto centers of foil. Top with remaining ingredients. Bring up foil sides. Double-fold top and ends to seal each packet, leaving room for heat circulation inside. Place in 15x10x1 inch baking pan. Bake 30 to 35 minutes or until chicken is cooked through. Let stand 5 minutes. Cut slits in foil to release steam before opening packets. Top each portion with 1 tablespoon of sour cream just before serving.

Garlic Pork Tenderloin

2	(1½ pound) pork tenderloins	1	tablespoon vegetable oil
1	(8 ounce) package fresh button mushrooms	2	teaspoons lemon pepper
2	red ripe tomatoes	2	teaspoons granulated garlic, divided
1	medium yellow onion	2	cups chicken stock
2	tablespoons flour	3	tablespoons cream
1	tablespoon butter		

Preheat oven to 350 degrees. Melt the butter and oil in a large, oven-safe pan with a lid. Season the pork with lemon pepper and half of the garlic. Roll the pork in the flour. Brown the pork on all sides over medium heat; this should take roughly 10 minutes. Remove the pork to a plate. While the pork is browning, bring a small pot of water to a boil and plunge the tomatoes in for 15 seconds. Rinse briefly and peel the skins off. Core, chop and set aside. Slice the onion and mushrooms. Once the pork is done, add the onions and mushrooms to the pan. Brown for 5 minutes, add the tomatoes, and stir to coat everything. Add the rest of the garlic and the chicken stock. Stir well. Place the pork back in the pan, cover and roast at 350 degrees for 45 to 60 minutes, until pork is done. Remove the pork from the pan add the cream to lightly thicken the sauce. It is only a bit of cream, and it makes a world of difference. But, if you don't wish to use it, once you have removed the pork, place the pan carefully back on the stovetop, and over medium-high heat, reduce the sauce by about ¼, at which point it will be thickened. Serve with pasta or rice. Serves 6 to 8.

Without a scoop of sorrow, our joy would not taste as sweet.

Slow Cooked
Baby Back Pork Ribs

6 pounds baby back ribs	barbecue sauce
¼ cup Dry Spice Rub	heavy duty aluminum foil

DRY SPICE RUB

½ cup chili powder	1 teaspoon salt
2 tablespoons sweet paprika	1 teaspoon pepper
½ tablespoon garlic powder	¼ teaspoon cayenne pepper
1 teaspoon onion powder	1 tablespoon sugar
½ teaspoon ground cumin	

Rinse ribs with cold water and pat dry. Mix all ingredients for spice rub and store in a tightly covered container in a dry place until ready for use. Rub dry spice rub into all surfaces of the ribs. Tear 2 pieces of heavy-duty aluminum foil into equal lengths, 12 inches longer than the length of the ribs. Place 2 pieces of foil on top of another one. Fold one long edge together several times and seal, pressing edges firmly to form a larger rectangle. Place the ribs in the center of one piece of foil. Fold the foil over top of the ribs. Again fold remaining 3 edges of the foil together pressing firmly to form a tightly sealed packet around the ribs. Place packet in a baking pan. (If you like you can let marinate 1 hour to 1 day.) Bake in a 300 degrees oven 3 to 4 hours. Remove ribs from oven; heat a charcoal grill to medium. Remove ribs from foil and grill over hot coals 15 to 20 minutes, while basting with your favorite barbecue sauce, being careful not to let ribs burn. Cut into serving size.

Pork Chops with Curry Apples

2   good sized boneless pork chops
½   teaspoon freshly ground black
    pepper
1   teaspoon sweet curry powder,
    divided
1   tablespoon vegetable oil

1   medium onion, peeled and diced
1   tablespoon cider vinegar
1   large apple, peeled and sliced
2   tablespoons water
¼   teaspoon salt

Wash the pork chops and pat dry. Trim off any excess fat, sprinkle with black pepper and half of the sweet curry powder. In a large heavy skillet, heat the vegetable oil over medium-high heat. Add the pork chops and cook for 3 to 5 minutes per side, depending on the thickness of the chops. Remove the chops from the pan when done; keep warm. Add the onions and sprinkle with remaining sweet curry powder. Deglaze the pan by adding the vinegar (it will bubble up right away); stir vigorously. Add the apples, toss to coat, add water, and cook until the apples are fairly tender. Don't cook them so long that they turn to mush, though they'll still taste great if that happens. Taste and add salt as desired. Spoon the sauce over the pork chops and serve with pasta or rice and a simple vegetable. Serves 2 to 3.

Tasty Garlic Shrimp

1   pound medium-large raw shrimp
    (21-30 count)
¼   cup butter
1   teaspoon minced or granulated
    garlic

½   teaspoon salt
¼   teaspoon black pepper
1   (8 ounce) package dry pasta
¼   teaspoon basil or oregano

Melt butter with the garlic, salt and pepper in a large saucepan over low heat. Start the water for the pasta. While the butter is melting, wash the shrimp, remove shell and vein (leave the tail), and rinse again. Cook the shrimp in a skillet over medium heat in 2 batches, until bright pink on both sides. The shrimp should be lightly curled; if they are tightly curled up they are too well done. Remove the first batch of the cooked shrimp to a platter; keep warm while cooking the second batch. Start cooking the pasta, according to the package instructions, a few minutes before starting the shrimp. Drain the cooked pasta and sprinkle with crumbled basil or oregano. Toss the shrimp and garlic butter with the pasta and serve immediately. Serves 4.

Salmon Croquettes

1	can salmon	3	tablespoons flour
2	tablespoons milk	⅛	teaspoon salt
1	egg	⅛	teaspoon pepper
¼	cup cornmeal		

Flake salmon, blend in eggs; stir in rest of ingredients. Shape into croquettes and fry in hot oil, turning once.

Herb Crusted Tilapia with Bow Tie Pasta

½	cup olive oil		bow tie pasta, prepared
½	teaspoon minced garlic		tilapia filets
1	red bell pepper, julienned	4	eggs, beaten
½	cup sweet corn		breadcrumbs
1	roma tomato, sliced		thyme
1	teaspoon basil		oregano

Sauté olive oil and garlic over medium heat. Add bell pepper and sauté until soft. Add corn, tomatoes and basil until flavors combine. Add prepared pasta and toss. Place pasta on plate. Dredge filets in egg wash then coat with breadcrumbs seasoned with thyme and oregano. Put fish into pan with heated olive oil. Brown on one side and place pan in 325 degrees oven until done. Place fish on top of pasta.

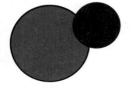

Smoked Fish Spread

1	pound wood smoked fish, amberjack or trout	1	bunch green onions, sliced
1½	cups mayonnaise		juice of 2 small lemons
		½	cup hot sauce to taste

Remove skin and bones from fish. Set aside. In a bowl combine mayonnaise, green onions, lemon juice, and hot sauce. Stir until well mixed. Add the fish and mix well. Transfer to an airtight container and refrigerate for at least 1 hour before serving. Makes 2 cups.

Grouper LaFitte

2	large eggs	1	tablespoon butter
1	cup milk	2	teaspoons minced garlic
2	cups all-purpose flour	¼	cup vermouth
1½	teaspoons Creole seasoning, divided	2	cups whipping cream
4	grouper fillets	¼	cup chopped green onions, divided
	vegetable oil	2	teaspoons lemon juice
12	large fresh shrimp, peeled and deveined	3	very thin slices cooked ham, cut into strips
			lemon slices, for garnish

Whisk together eggs and milk in a shallow dish. Combine flour and 1 teaspoon Creole seasoning in another shallow dish. Dredge fillets in flour mixture, dip in egg mixture, and dredge in flour again. Pour oil (about 3 inches deep) into a heavy large skillet and heat to 360 degrees. Fry grouper fillets 6 minutes or until golden brown. Drain on clean brown paper bags. Keep fish warm in the oven set on warm. Melt butter in a heavy large skillet over medium heat. Add shrimp and minced garlic and cook, stirring often until shrimp turn pink. Remove shrimp and reserve drippings left in skillet. Stir vermouth into reserved drippings, bring mixture to a boil, and cook 1 minute. Add whipping cream, 2 tablespoons green onions, lemon juice, and ½ teaspoon Creole seasoning. Cook, stirring often, about 12 to 15 minutes or until mixture thickens. To serve, place grouper fillets on a serving platter, drizzle with sauce. Top with shrimp and ham and sprinkle with remaining green onions. Garnish with lemon slices, if desired. Serves 6.

Baked Cornish Hens with Vegetables

2	Cornish hens, split lengthwise	2	tablespoons rosemary
3	tablespoons lemon juice	2	small onions, quartered
3	tablespoons olive oil	2	cups baby carrots
1	teaspoon garlic powder	8	red potatoes, quartered

Place hens, skin side up, in greased baking dish. Combine lemon juice, olive oil, rosemary, and garlic and spoon on evenly. Place vegetables around hens and bake, uncovered, at 450 degrees for 35 to 40 minutes.

Sweet Onion Sirloin

1	medium onion, very thinly sliced	¼	cup water
1	boneless beef top sirloin steak (about 1 pound)	2	tablespoons Worcestershire sauce
		1	tablespoon sugar

Lightly coat 12-inch skillet with nonstick cooking spray; heat over high heat until hot. Add onion; cook and stir 4 minutes or until browned. Remove from skillet and set aside. Wipe out skillet with paper towel. Coat same skillet with additional cooking spray; heat until hot. Add beef; cook 10 to 13 minutes for medium-rare to medium, turning once. Remove from heat and transfer to cutting board; let stand 3 minutes before slicing. Meanwhile, return skillet to high heat until hot; add onion, water, Worcestershire sauce and sugar. Cook 30 to 45 seconds or until most liquid had evaporated. Thinly slice beef on the diagonal and serve with onions.

Pork and Plum Kabobs

¾ pound boneless pork loin chops
  (1 inch thick), trimmed of fat and
  cut into 1 inch pieces
1½ teaspoons ground cumin
½ teaspoon ground cinnamon
¼ teaspoon salt
¼ teaspoon garlic powder

¼ teaspoon ground red pepper
¼ cup no-sugar-added red raspberry
  spread
¼ cup sliced green onions
1 tablespoon orange juice
3 plums, pitted and cut into wedges

Place pork in large resealable plastic food storage bag. Combine cumin, cinnamon, salt, garlic powder and red pepper in small bowl. Sprinkle over meat in bag. Shake to coat meat with spices. Lightly coat grill grid with nonstick cooking spray. Prepare grill for direct grilling. Combine raspberry spread, green onions and orange juice in small bowl; set aside. Alternately thread pork and plum wedges onto 8 skewers. Grill kabobs directly over medium heat 12 to 14 minutes or until meat is barely pink in the center, turning once during grilling. Brush frequently with reserved raspberry mixture during last 5 minutes of grilling.

Grilled Herbed Chicken

½ cup chopped onion
⅓ cup lime juice
6 cloves garlic, coarsely chopped
1 teaspoon dried oregano
1 teaspoon ground cumin

½ teaspoon dried thyme
¼ teaspoon ground red pepper
6 boneless skinless chicken breasts
3 tablespoons chopped fresh
  cilantro

Combine onion, lime juice and garlic in food processor. Process until onion is finely minced. Transfer to resealable plastic food storage bag. Add oregano, cumin, thyme and red pepper; knead bag until blended. Place chicken in bag; press out air and seal. Turn to coat chicken with marinade. Refrigerate 30 minutes or up to 4 hours. Lightly coat grill grid with nonstick cooking spray. Prepare grill for direct cooking. Remove chicken from marinade; discard marinade. Place chicken on grid 3 to 4 inches from medium-hot coals. Grill 5 to 7 minutes on each side or until chicken is no longer pink in center. Transfer to clean serving platter and sprinkle with cilantro.

Grilled Chicken with Spicy Black Beans & Rice

1 boneless skinless chicken breast (about ¼ pound)
½ teaspoon Caribbean jerk seasoning
½ teaspoon olive oil
¼ cup finely diced green bell pepper
2 teaspoons chipotle chili powder
¾ cup hot cooked rice

½ cup rinsed and drained canned black beans
2 tablespoons diced pimiento
1 tablespoon chopped pimiento-stuffed green olives
1 tablespoon chopped onion
1 tablespoon chopped fresh cilantro (optional)
lime wedges for garnish.

Lightly coat grill grid with nonstick cooking spray. Prepare grill for direct grilling. Rub chicken with jerk seasoning. Grill over medium-hot coals 8 to 10 minutes or until no longer pink in center. Meanwhile, heat oil in medium saucepan or skillet over medium heat. Add bell pepper and chili powder; cook and stir until peppers are soft. Add rice, beans, pimiento and olives to saucepan. Cook about 3 minutes or until hot. Serve bean mixture with chicken. Top bean mixture with onion and cilantro, if desired. Garnish with lime wedges, if desired.

Tuna-Stuffed Tomatoes

6 medium tomatoes
1 cup dry-curd cottage cheese
½ cup plain low-fat yogurt
1 (6½ ounce) can tuna, packed in water, drained and flaked
¼ cup chopped cucumber
¼ cup chopped green bell pepper

¼ cup thinly sliced radishes
¼ cup chopped green onions
½ teaspoon dried basil leaves, crushed
⅛ teaspoon garlic powder
lettuce leaves

Cut each tomato into 6 wedges, cutting to, but not through, base of each tomato. Refrigerate. In medium bowl, combine cottage cheese and yogurt; mix well. Stir in remaining ingredients except lettuce leaves. Place tomatoes on individual lettuce-lined plates; spread wedges apart. Spoon cottage cheese mixture into center of each tomato.

Southwest Roasted Salmon and Corn

2	medium ears fresh corn, unhusked	¼	teaspoon ground cumin
1	(6 ounce) salmon fillet, cut into 2 equal pieces	¼	teaspoon dried oregano
		⅛	teaspoon salt, divided
1	tablespoon plus 1 teaspoon fresh lime juice, divided	⅛	teaspoon black pepper
		2	teaspoons margarine, melted
1	clove garlic, minced	2	teaspoons minced fresh cilantro
½	teaspoon chili powder		

Pull back husks from each ear of corn, leaving husks attached. Discard silk. Bring husks back up over each ear. Soak corn in cold water 20 minutes. Preheat oven to 400 degrees. Lightly coat shallow 1-quart baking dish with nonstick cooking spray. Place salmon, skin side down, in prepared dish. Pour 1 tablespoon lime juice over salmon. Marinate at room temperature 15 minutes. Combine garlic, chili powder, cumin, oregano, half of salt and the pepper in small bowl. Pat salmon lightly with paper towel. Rub garlic mixture on tops and sides of salmon. Remove corn from water. Place corn on one side of oven rack. Roast 10 minutes. Turn. Place salmon, in baking dish on other side of oven rack. Roast 15 minutes or until salmon is opaque and flakes when tested with fork, and corn is tender. Combine margarine, cilantro, remaining 1 teaspoon lime juice and remaining salt in small bowl. Remove husks from corn. Brush margarine mixture over corn. Serve corn with salmon.

One Dish Dinner

½	pound mild sausage	1	large onion, chopped
½	pound chuck or very lean hamburger meat	1	can cream of mushroom soup
		1	large can mushrooms (optional)
½	pound Velveeta cheese, cubed	2	cups macaroni, cooked

Brown and chop hamburger meat, sausage and onion. Drain fat. Pour all ingredients in a casserole dish and bake at 350 degrees for 20 minutes or until cheese is bubbly.

Chicken Divan

1 boneless chicken breast, cooked
1 (10 ounce) package frozen broccoli
1 (10½ ounce) can cream of chicken
    soup
¼ cup water
2 ounces (¼ cup) American or sharp
    cheese, shredded
2 tablespoons bread crumbs

Slice chicken breast. Cook broccoli in small amount of water until tender; drain. Lay broccoli in greased baking dish. Arrange chicken slices on top. Add water to soup and pour over. Sprinkle cheese on top, then crumbs. Bake at 350 degrees until heated through and cheese is melted.

Spectacular Chicken Casserole

3 cups cooked white chicken, diced
1 can cream of celery soup
1 (16 ounce) can French-cut green
    beans
1 (4 ounce) jar sliced mushrooms,
    drained
1 package wild long grain rice
1 large can French fried onions
1 cup mayonnaise
    salt and pepper to taste

Mix in bowl. Pour in buttered casserole dish and bake 30 minutes at 350 degrees or freeze and bake later. Use ½ of onions in recipe. Put other ½ of onions on top last 5 minutes of cooking.

Breakfast Casserole

1 pound sausage, cooked and
    scrambled
6 slices white bread
1 cup grated Cheddar cheese
2 cups milk
5 eggs
1 teaspoon each: salt and dry
    mustard (mixed together)

Fry and scramble sausage; drain. Cut crust from bread and discard. Butter both sides of bread and cut into cubes. Spread buttered bread cubes on bottom of 9x13x2-inch casserole dish. Top with sausage. Cover completely with grated cheese. Mix remaining ingredients together; beat well. Pour liquid over top of cheese, sausage and bread. Refrigerate at least 8 hours. Bake at 350 degrees for 40 to 50 minutes or until browned slightly.

Breakfast Quiche

2	9-inch pie shells	6	eggs
1	pound sausage	¾	cup milk
1	medium onion, chopped		salt and pepper to taste
8	ounces shredded Cheddar cheese		

Brown sausage and onion. Drain. Combine everything and put in pie shells. Bake at 350 degrees for 35 to 40 minutes.

Beef Barbecue

BBQ

2	pounds beef	2	cups diced celery
2	onions		

SAUCE

2	cups broth	1	tablespoon Worcestershire sauce
1	bottle ketchup	1	tablespoon brown sugar
1	tablespoon vinegar	1	teaspoon salt
1	tablespoon lemon juice	½	teaspoon dry mustard

Cook beef, onions and celery on medium heat until tender enough to shred the meat. Cook sauce ingredients on low heat for 10 minutes, then add to meat and simmer 10 minutes longer.

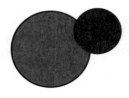

Santa Fe Chicken

1½ pounds chicken breasts, cut into strips
1 teaspoon paprika
1 teaspoon salt
¼ teaspoon pepper
2 tablespoons olive oil or butter
1 medium onion, chopped
1 small green pepper, chopped
1 clove garlic, minced
1 can chicken broth
1 (10 ounce) can Rotel tomatoes
1½ cups instant rice
1 cup shredded Monterey cheese

Cook chicken for 2 minutes in oil. Add onion, green pepper and garlic; cook until tender, about 4 minutes. Drain tomatoes. Reserve liquid. Add enough chicken broth to tomato liquid to equal 1½ cups. Add liquid to skillet; bring to a boil. Stir in rice. Cover and remove from heat. Let stand until all liquid is absorbed, about 5 minutes. Sprinkle with cheese.

Ranch Chicken

¾ cup crushed cornflakes
¾ cup grated Parmesan cheese
1 envelope ranch salad dressing mix
2 pounds boneless skinless chicken breast halves
½ cup butter or margarine, melted

In a shallow bowl, combine the cornflakes, Parmesan cheese and salad dressing mix. Dip chicken in butter, then roll in cornflake mixture until coated. Place in a greased 9x13-inch baking dish. Bake, uncovered, at 350 degrees for 45 minutes or until juices run clear.

Pecan Chicken

2½ teaspoons poultry seasoning
1½ teaspoons salt
4 chicken breasts
½ cup brown sugar
½ cup maple flavored syrup
1 cup chopped pecans

Combine poultry seasoning and salt in small bowl, set aside. Lay chicken breast in sprayed 9x13-inch baking dish. Sprinkle each breast with 1 teaspoon of the seasoning mix. In a small mixing bowl combine brown sugar, syrup and pecans. Top each breast with ½ cup of the pecan mixture. Bake at 400 degrees for 20 to 30 minutes or until juices in chicken run clear when pierced.

Beef Tips and Rice

2 pounds beef tips
1 can cream of mushroom soup
1 can cream of chicken soup
2 cans water

2 packages onion or mushroom soup mix
cooked rice

In casserole dish roll meat in onion/mushroom mix. Pour soup and water over meat and mix well. Cover. Bake at 350 degrees for 3 hours. Serve over rice.

Delicious Meat Loaf

3 pounds ground chuck
1 egg
½-¾ cup bread crumbs
1 package onion and mushroom soup mix

1 (8 ounce) can tomato sauce
1 teaspoon Worcestershire sauce
1 pinch salt and pepper
ketchup

Combine all ingredients together and form into a loaf; bake in a 9x13-inch baking dish. Bake at 350 degrees for 1 hour and 15 minutes. Spread ketchup on top of meat and bake 15 minutes longer.

Easy Lasagna

1 pound ground beef or Italian sausage
1 (32 ounce) jar thick spaghetti sauce
1½ cups water
2 (15 ounce) packages ricotta or cottage cheese
3 cups shredded mozzarella cheese

½ cup grated Parmesan cheese
2 eggs
¼ cup chopped parsley
1 teaspoon salt
¼ teaspoon pepper
8 ounces uncooked lasagna

Brown beef in 3 quart saucepan; drain off fat. Add sauce and water. Simmer about 10 minutes. Combine remaining ingredients, except lasagna. Pour about 1 cup sauce on bottom of 9x13-inch baking dish. Layer 3 pieces of uncooked lasagna over sauce. Cover with about 1½ cups of sauce. Layer ½ of the cheese filling over the sauce. Repeat layers of lasagna, sauce and cheese filling. Top with a layer of lasagna and remaining sauce. Cover with aluminum foil and bake at 350 degrees for 50 to 60 minutes. Remove foil and bake 10 minutes longer. Allow to stand 10 minutes before cutting. Makes 8 to 10 servings.

Poulet de Normandy

1 (16 ounce) package herb seasoned stuffing mix
1 stick margarine, melted
¼ cup green onions with tops
½ cup chopped celery
2½ cups diced chicken or turkey
1 can cream of mushroom soup

1½ cups hot broth
½ cup mayonnaise
¾ teaspoon salt
2 eggs
1½ cups milk
grated cheese, mild

Mix stuffing and margarine and set aside. Combine onions, celery, mayonnaise and salt. Mix well with stuffing mixture. In greased 9x13-inch baking dish, put half of stuffing mixture, then spread chicken; top with rest of stuffing mixture. Beat eggs in milk, pour over all. Refrigerate overnight. Take out 2 hours before serving and spread with mushroom soup. Bake uncovered at 325 degrees for 40 minutes. Sprinkle with grated cheese and bake 10 minutes longer.

Chicken Taco Pie

1½-2 pounds chicken
1 large can enchilada sauce
1 can cream of mushroom soup
1 large onion, chopped
½ teaspoon garlic salt

dash of pepper
1 large package corn chips
1 cup cheese, grated
1 cup chicken broth

Boil chicken until tender. Remove bones and cut into bite-size pieces. Combine chicken, enchilada sauce, mushroom soup, onion, garlic salt and pepper. Grease baking dish, line with corn chips. Add chicken mixture. Sprinkle with grated cheese, cover with corn chips. Add chicken broth. Bake at 350 degrees for 30 minutes.

Chicken–Cashew Casserole

¼ cup chopped onion
1 cup finely diced celery
1 pound butter
1 can mushroom soup
⅓ cup chicken broth
1 teaspoon soy sauce

3 drops hot pepper sauce
⅛ teaspoon pepper
2 cups diced cooked chicken
1 cup chow mein noodles
⅓ cup cashew nuts

Sauté the onions and celery in butter. Add the soup and chicken broth. Season with soy sauce, hot pepper sauce and pepper. Add the chicken and simmer a few minutes. Pour into a 1 quart casserole dish; sprinkle with chow mein noodles and cashew nuts. Bake at 350 degrees for 20 minutes until bubbly. Serves 6.

Chicken Pot Pie

1 chicken
2 tablespoons butter
1 small onion, chopped
2 tablespoons flour
⅛ teaspoon thyme
  salt and pepper to taste

½ cup chicken broth or bouillon cube, dissolved in ½ cup water
½ cup milk
  lemon juice
  Worcestershire sauce
1 can Veg-All or mixed vegetables
  Bisquick

Cook and debone chicken. Melt butter on low heat. Add chopped onion, flour, thyme, salt and pepper to taste. Add chicken, 2 teaspoons lemon juice and a dash of Worcestershire. Mix well. Add chicken broth and milk. Heat until almost boiling. Remove from heat and add vegetables. Pour into casserole dish and cover with Bisquick crust to fit size of bowl. Bake at 350 degrees until crust is golden brown.

One Pot Supper

6	pork chops	½	cup water
1	can tomato soup	1	teaspoon Worcestershire sauce
½	teaspoon salt	3	medium potatoes
4	small carrots		

Quarter potatoes and split carrots lengthwise. In skillet, brown pork chops. Pour off fat. Add remaining ingredients. Cover and simmer 45 minutes or until vegetables are tender. Stir frequently.

Hamburger Tot Casserole

1	pound hamburger, cooked and drained	1	can cream of celery or mushroom soup
1	package dry onion soup mix	1	package tater tots
1	can English peas, drained		

In a casserole dish, layer the above ingredients as listed. Bake at 350 degrees for about 45 minutes to 1 hour.

Greek Spaghetti

1	pound Velveeta	2	cans Rotel
1	pound spaghetti	2	tablespoons Greek seasoning
2	(12 ounce) cans canned chicken		

Boil noodles on stove until done. While cooking noodles, cut Velveeta into cubes and put into large bowl with other ingredients. Place ingredients in microwave and cook until cheese is melted completely. When noodles are done, drain and pour into bowl of sauce. Toss well and serve.

Coconut Fried Shrimp

1¼ cups all-purpose flour
1¼ cups cornstarch
6½ teaspoons baking powder
½ teaspoon salt
¼ teaspoon Cajun seasoning
1½ cups cold water
½ teaspoon vegetable oil

2½ cups flaked coconut
1 pound uncooked large shrimp,
    peeled and deveined
    additional oil for deep-fat frying
1 cup orange marmalade
¼ cup honey

In a small bowl, combine the first five ingredients. Stir in water and oil until smooth. Place coconut in another bowl. Dip shrimp into batter, then coat with coconut. In an electric skillet or deep-fat fryer, heat oil to 375 degrees. Fry shrimp, a few at a time, for 3 minutes or until golden brown. Drain on paper towels. In a saucepan, heat marmalade and honey; stir until blended. Serve as a dipping sauce for the shrimp. Serves 4.

Dilly Pork Chops

6 boneless pork loin chops
    (½ inch thick)
¼ cup butter, melted
1 tablespoon Dijon mustard

1-1½ teaspoons dill weed
1 teaspoon Worcestershire sauce
⅛ teaspoon garlic powder

Prick pork chops with a fork. In a small bowl, combine the remaining ingredients; spoon over both sides of chops. Place on broiler pan; broil 4 to 6 inches from the heat for 4 minutes on each side or until juices run clear.

Citrus Grilled Salmon

½   cup orange juice
½   cup honey
2   teaspoons prepared horseradish

2   teaspoons teriyaki sauce
1   teaspoon grated orange peel
1   salmon fillet (about 2½ pounds)

In a small bowl, combine the first five ingredients; mix well. Pour ⅔ cup into a large resealable plastic bag; add salmon. Seal bag and turn to coat; refrigerate for at least 2 hours. Cover and refrigerate remaining marinade. Coat grill rack with nonstick cooking spray before starting the grill. Drain and discard marinade from salmon. Place salmon skin side down on grill rack. Grill, covered, over medium heat for 5 minutes. Brush with some of the reserved marinade. Grill 10 to 15 minutes longer or until fish flakes easily with a fork, basting occasionally with remaining marinade. Makes 6 to 8 servings.

Baked Parmesan Fish

⅓   cup grated Parmesan cheese
2   tablespoons all-purpose flour
½   teaspoon paprika
¼   teaspoon salt
⅛   teaspoon pepper

1   egg
2   tablespoons milk
4   orange roughy or catfish fillets
    (4 ounces each)

In a shallow bowl, combine the Parmesan cheese, flour, paprika, salt and pepper. In another shallow bowl, beat egg and milk. Dip fish fillets into egg mixture, then coat with the Parmesan mixture. Arrange in a greased 9x13-inch baking dish. Bake, uncovered, at 350 degrees for 25 to 30 minutes or until fish flakes easily with a fork.

Glorious Shrimp

3 pounds medium to large white shrimp, peeled and deveined
½ pound butter, melted
2 cloves garlic, crushed
½ teaspoon paprika
½ teaspoon sea salt
½ teaspoon cayenne pepper
2 cups soft breadcrumbs
⅓ cup chopped fresh parsley

Preheat oven to 350 degrees. Rinse peeled and deveined shrimp, drain, and pat dry. Mix together butter, garlic, paprika, salt, and cayenne pepper. Set the butter mixture aside. Use the food processor fitted with the steel blade to make breadcrumbs. Add parsley to bread crumbs and mix well. Toss shrimp and bread crumb mixture in a large bowl. Arrange shrimp in a buttered 9x13 inch baking dish. Pour butter mixture over shrimp. Bake 20 to 30 minutes, or until bubbly. Stir half way through baking. Serves 8 to 10.

Lemon Scampi

2 pounds fresh, large shrimp
½ cup butter or margarine
4 cloves garlic, crushed
4 tablespoons lemon juice
1 teaspoon lemon zest
dash hot sauce
½ teaspoon salt
1 tablespoon finely chopped green onion
¼ cup chopped fresh parsley, optional

Peel and devein shrimp. Set aside. Melt butter in a large skillet; sauté garlic for 30 seconds just until garlic releases its aroma. Remove from heat and add lemon juice, zest, hot sauce and salt. Toss with shrimp. Preheat oven to 350 degrees. Arrange shrimp with lemon sauce in a single layer in a 9x13 inch pan. Top with green onions. Bake 15 minutes until shrimp turns pink and cooked through. Remove from oven and toss with parsley. Serves 6.

Crab Quiche

1	(9 inch) pie crust	1	(2 ounce) jar diced pimentos, drained
1	(6 ounce) can white crabmeat, drained	3	large eggs
1	cup shredded Swiss cheese	1	cup milk or half & half
¼	cup grated Parmesan cheese	½	teaspoon salt
¼	cup chopped green onions	⅛	teaspoon pepper

Preheat oven to 350 degrees. Press pie crust into a pie pan. In even layers place crabmeat, Swiss cheese, Parmesan cheese, onion and pimento into pie crust. In a small bowl, beat eggs with milk, salt and pepper. Pour over layers. Bake 45 to 50 minutes or until a knife inserted halfway between side and center comes out clean. Remove from oven and let stand 10 minutes before cutting. Serves 6.

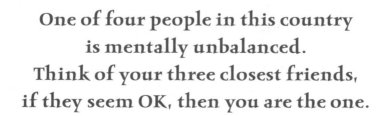

**One of four people in this country
is mentally unbalanced.
Think of your three closest friends,
if they seem OK, then you are the one.**

Taste of Desserts

Strawberry Cake

1	strawberry cake mix	1	cup fresh or frozen strawberries
1	(3 ounce) box instant vanilla pudding	1	cup chopped pecans
½	(3 ounce) box strawberry gelatin	1	cup coconut
1	(8 ounce) container sour cream	3	tablespoons self-rising flour
½	cup water	1	(8 ounce) package cream cheese
½	cup vegetable oil	1	stick margarine
4	eggs	½	(3 ounce) box strawberry gelatin
		1	box confectioners' sugar

Combine cake mix, pudding mix, gelatin, sour cream, water, oil and eggs; mix for 2 minutes. Combine strawberries, pecans, coconut and flour, coating well. Add to cake mix. Pour into one tube pan sprayed with nonstick cooking spray. Bake at 325 degrees for 65 minutes. Can be put into 3 layer cake pans. Bake at 350 degrees for 28 to 30 minutes. Beat cream cheese and margarine together. Add gelatin, beat well. Add confectioners' sugar and beat for 2 minutes. Spread on cooled cake.

Orange Pound Cake

1	orange flavored cake mix	1	(8 ounce) package sour cream
1	(3 ounce) box instant vanilla pudding	1	(8 ounce) can crushed pineapple with juice
½	(3 ounce) box orange gelatin	1	(8 ounce) package cream cheese
4	eggs	1	stick margarine
1	(11 ounce) can Mandarin oranges, drained	½	(3 ounce) box orange gelatin
		1	box confectioners' sugar

Mix cake mix, pudding mix, gelatin, oil, eggs, oranges, sour cream, undrained pineapple, beat for 2 minutes. Pour into one tube pan sprayed with non-stick cooking spray. Bake at 325 degrees for 65 minutes. Can be baked into 3 layer cake pans. Bake at 350 degrees for 28 to 30 minutes. Beat cream cheese and margarine together. Add gelatin and beat well. Add confectioners' sugar and beat for 2 minutes. Spread on cooled cake.

Upside Down German Chocolate Cake

1 cup chopped pecans
1 small can coconut
1 German chocolate cake mix

1 (8 ounce) package cream cheese
1 box confectioners' sugar
1 stick margarine

Sprinkle chopped pecans on bottom of greased 10x14 inch pan. Sprinkle coconut over pecans. Mix the cake mix according to directions on box. Pour slowly over pecans and coconut. In a mixing bowl, mix softened cream cheese and margarine. Add confectioners' sugar slowly while mixing. Some lumps will remain. Pour mixture slowly over cake batter. Preheat oven to 350 degrees and bake for 40 minutes.

Fresh Apple Cake

2 cups flour
3 teaspoons cinnamon
1 teaspoon salt
2 tablespoons baking powder
1½ cups vegetable oil
2 cups sugar
4 eggs

3 cups chopped apple
1 cup chopped black walnuts
1 (3 ounce) package cream cheese
¼ cup margarine
1 box confectioners' sugar
1 teaspoon vanilla extract

Sift together dry ingredients. In a large bowl combine oil, sugar, and eggs. Add dry ingredients. Fold in apples and nuts. Bake in a greased Bundt pan or 9x13 inch pan in a 350 degrees oven for 40 to 50 minutes. Mix cream cheese, margarine, confectioners' sugar and vanilla extract, frost cake.

Chess Cake

1   box yellow cake mix
3   eggs, divided
1   stick butter, melted

1   cup chopped pecans
1   box confectioners' sugar
1   (8 ounce) package cream cheese

Mix cake mix, 1 egg and butter together and press into a well greased and floured 9x13 inch pan. Mix 2 eggs and cream cheese well. Add confectioners' sugar and mix well. Pour over top of cake mix. Add pecans, if desired. Bake at 350 degrees for about 45 minutes.

Easy Holiday Cake

1   prepared angel food cake
1   package fresh or frozen
      strawberries

1   carton vanilla ice cream,
      softened

Pour the strawberries into the center hole of the angel food cake. Spread the ice cream over the top of the cake. Re-freeze.

Blueberry Dump Cake

3   cups fresh blueberries
1   can crushed pineapple with juice

1   box white or yellow cake mix
2   sticks melted butter

Preheat oven to 350 degrees. Spray Pam in a 9x13 inch pan. Dump ingredients in order (yes, dump in the dry cake mix) and bake for 40 to 45 minutes.

Caramel Apple Cheesecake

1   (21 ounce) can apple fruit filling, divided
1   (9 inch) graham cracker crust
2   (8 ounce) packages cream cheese, softened
½   cup sugar
¼   teaspoon vanilla extract
2   eggs
    apple slices
¼   cup caramel topping
12 pecans halves
2   tablespoons chopped pecans

Reserve ¾ cup apple filling. Spoon remaining filling into crust. Beat together cream cheese, sugar and vanilla extract until smooth. Add eggs and beat well. Pour over apple filling Bake 35 minutes at 350 degrees or until center is set. Cool. Mix reserved apple filling and caramel topping in a small saucepan. Heat about 1 minute. Arrange apple slices around outside edge of cheesecake. Spoon caramel topping onto the cheesecake and spread evenly. Decorate with pecan halves around the edge. Sprinkle with chopped pecans. Refrigerate until ready to serve.

Peach Cake

3   cups flour
1½   cups sugar
¾   cup margarine
1½   teaspoons baking powder
1   teaspoon baking soda
1   teaspoon ginger
1   teaspoon cinnamon
½   teaspoon cloves
½   teaspoon salt
2   eggs
1½   cups sour milk
1   can sliced peaches

Blend flour, sugar and margarine until crumbly and reserve 1½ cups. Mix remainder with rest of the ingredients. Spread ½ of the crumbs in greased 9 x 13 inch pan, pour in batter, top with can sliced peaches and rest of crumbs. Bake at 350 degrees for 45 to 50 minutes.

Cherry Dump Cake

1   can cherry pie filling
1   (16 ounce) can pineapple, crushed
1   package Duncan Hines Yellow
      Cake Mix

2   sticks margarine, melted
½   cup chopped pecans
½   cup coconut

Grease 9x13 inch pan and add in this order; cherry pie filling, pineapple, then cover with cake mix, butter, sprinkle nuts and coconut. Bake 350 degrees for 50 minutes.

Funnel Cakes

3   cups unsifted flour
1   teaspoon baking powder
3   eggs
1   teaspoon vanilla extract

¼   cup sugar
½   teaspoon salt
2   cups milk

Mix eggs, sugar, milk and vanilla extract; add flour and salt. Run batter through funnel into hot oil making crooked lines. Fry as doughnuts. Sprinkle with confectioners' sugar.

Blessed are those who
hunger and thirst
for they are sticking to their diets.

Red Velvet Cake

2½ cups sugar
¾ cup shortening
2 eggs
2 tablespoons cocoa
1 ounce red food coloring

1 tablespoon baking soda
1 teaspoon salt
1 tablespoon vanilla extract
1½ cups buttermilk

Cream sugar, shortening, eggs, cocoa, and food coloring. In another bowl mix soda, salt, and vanilla extract. Combine mixtures and add alternately with buttermilk and flour. Divide into 3 (8 inch) layers. Bake at 350 degrees for 30 to 35 minutes.

ICING FOR RED VELVET CAKE

1½ cups milk
6 tablespoons flour

1½ cups sugar
1½ cups shortening

Cook milk and flour until thick and set aside to cool. Mix sugar and shortening until creamy and add to cooled mixture. Beat real good and spread between layers and on top.

Hummingbird Cake

3 cups all-purpose flour
2 cups sugar
1 teaspoon salt
1 teaspoon cinnamon
3 eggs, beaten
½ cup vegetable oil
1½ teaspoons vanilla extract
1 (20 ounce) can chopped pineapple with juice

2 cups sliced bananas
2 cups chopped pecans
1 (8 ounce) package cream cheese
½ stick softened margarine
1 (16 ounce) box confectioners' sugar
1 teaspoon vanilla extract

Combine dry ingredients in a large bowl. Add eggs and oil; stir until moist. Stir in vanilla extract, pineapple with the juice, bananas and pecans. Spray large, rectangular baking pan liberally with Pam. Spoon batter into pan. Bake at 350 degrees for 45 to 50 minutes. Cool completely. For icing: combine softened cream cheese, margarine and vanilla extract. Add confectioners' sugar in slowly, beat until smooth. Spread over cooled cake. Decorate top with pecan halves if desired.

Lemonade Cake

1   box Duncan Hines Lemon Supreme cake mix, prepared as directed
1   small can frozen lemonade, thawed
1   (14 ounce) can sweetened condensed milk
1   (12 ounce) container Cool Whip

Preheat oven to 350 degrees. Bake cake, as directed on box in 2 (8 inch) pans. Cool completely. Stir together the frozen lemonade and sweetened condensed milk. Fold in Cool Whip. Frost the 2 layer cake, generously. Keep in refrigerator at least 2 hours before serving.

Lemon Supreme Cake

1   package Duncan Hines Lemon Supreme cake mix
½   cup sugar
½   cup oil
4   eggs
1   cup apricot nectar

Mix all ingredients together in large mixing bowl. Pour into a greased tube pan. Bake at 350 degrees for 1 hour. Glaze: 1 cup confectioners' sugar, 2 tablespoons lemon juice. Drizzle over cake after it has cooled for 15 to 20 minutes.

Cream Cheese Pound Cake

1   (8 ounce) package cream cheese
3   cups flour, sifted (½ all-purpose and ½ cake flour)
3   cups sugar
3   sticks butter
1   teaspoon vanilla extract
1   teaspoon almond flavoring
6   eggs

Cream the cheese and butter until light. Add sugar and cream until very light and fluffy. Add eggs, one at a time. Add vanilla extract and almond flavoring. Add flour, a little at a time. Grease and flour Bundt pan. Bake at 325 degrees for 1½ hours.

Tropical Cake

1 box yellow cake mix	1½ cups heavy cream
1 (20 ounce) can crushed pineapple	1 cup flaked, sweetened toasted
1½ cups sugar, divided	coconut
1 box French vanilla pudding	

Preheat oven to 350 degrees. Prepare yellow cake mix as directed using a greased 9x13 inch pan and bake for 30 to 35 minutes. While cake is baking, combine the pineapple and 1 cup of sugar in a saucepan, and bring to a boil over medium heat stirring constantly. Remove from heat and allow to cool slightly. Remove cake from oven and using a fork, pierce holes into cake. Pour pineapple mixture over hot cake and set aside. Prepare pudding according to package directions. Spread pudding over cake and refrigerate until thoroughly chilled. Whip heavy cream and remaining sugar until stiff. Cover top of cake with whipped cream and sprinkle toasted coconut on top.

Quick Coffee Cake

1½ cups flour	½ cup milk
2½ teaspoons baking powder	3 tablespoons flour
¼ teaspoon salt	1 teaspoon cinnamon
¾ cup sugar	¼ cup sugar
¼ cup Crisco	2 tablespoons butter, softened
1 egg	

Cream Crisco and ¾ cup of sugar together in a bowl. Add 1½ cups of flour, powder, salt, eggs, and milk together with Crisco mix. Place in 8x8 inch pan. Topping: mix together butter, cinnamon, 3 tablespoons of flour, and ¼ cup of sugar until crumbly. Sprinkle over top of cake batter. Bake at 375 degrees for 25 to 30 minutes. Serve warm with butter.

Carrot Cake

1½ cups oil
2   cups sugar
4   large eggs, well beaten
2   cups plain flour

2   teaspoons baking soda
2   teaspoons cinnamon
2   teaspoons baking powder
3   cups grated carrots

Mix oil and sugar; beat well. Add beaten eggs. Sift dry ingredients 3 times. Add to other mixture and mix well. Last, add grated carrots, small amount at a time. Bake in 3 layers in 350 degree oven for 35 minutes or until done. Grease pans and use wax paper.

Cherry Cheese Cake

1   stick margarine
1½ cups graham cracker crumbs
½   cup sugar
1   cup powdered sugar

1   (8 ounce) package cream cheese, softened
1   can cherry pie filling
1   container whipped topping

Mix margarine, crumbs and sugar and place in bottom of large baking dish. Bake 5 minutes at 325 degrees; let cool. Mix powdered sugar with cream cheese; spread over cracker crumbs. Put cherry pie filling on cream cheese. Top with whipped topping.

Strange Cake

1   box cake mix (any flavor)
4   eggs
1   stick and 1 tablespoon butter, melted and divided

1   box powdered sugar
1   (8 ounce) package cream cheese

Mix dry cake mix, 2 eggs and 1 stick melted butter together; makes stiff dough. Press into greased and floured 9x13-inch baking dish, making a ridge around the top. Set aside. Mix powdered sugar, remaining 2 eggs, cream cheese and 1 tablespoon melted butter. Pour over cake mixture. Bake at 350 degrees for 30 minutes.

Apple Dapple Cake

CAKE

1½ cups oil	1 teaspoon soda
2 cups sugar	1 teaspoon salt
3 large eggs	3 cups fresh chopped apples
2 teaspoon vanilla	1 cup chopped pecans
3 cups all-purpose flour	

SAUCE

1 cup brown sugar	¼ cup milk
1 stick margarine	

Mix oil, sugar, eggs and vanilla well; sift dry ingredients together and blend with egg mixture. Stir in apples and nuts. Bake at 325 degrees until done. For sauce, mix all ingredients and cook for 3 minutes; pour over cake and let set 2 hours before serving.

7-Up Cake

CAKE

1 box lemon supreme cake mix	¾ cup oil
1 box instant pineapple pudding mix	1 (10 ounce) bottle 7-Up
4 eggs	

ICING

1½ cup sugar	1 stick margarine
1 tablespoon flour	1 small can crushed pineapple
2 eggs	1 cup coconut

Combine cake mix and pudding mix; add oil and mix well. Add eggs one at a time mixing thoroughly. Stir in 7-Up; bake in 3 layers or sheet pan 25 to 30 minutes at 350 degrees. For icing, cook sugar, flour, eggs and pineapple until thickened. Add coconut and spread between layers and on top of cake.

Texas Punch Bowl Cake

1 box yellow butter recipe cake mix (bake according to directions on box)
2 large packages frozen strawberries with juice, thawed
5 bananas
2 large boxes instant vanilla pudding mix
6 cups milk
1 large can crushed pineapple, undrained
1 large tub Cool Whip
1 can coconut
½ cup chopped nuts for topping (optional)
cherries (optional)

Using a small punch bowl, add ½ of cake (tear or cut to fit punch bowl). Dump 1 package frozen strawberries over cake. Slice 2 ½ bananas over strawberries. In large bowl, combine pudding mixes with milk until well blended. Spread ½ of vanilla pudding over bananas. Pour ½ can of crushed pineapple with juice over the pudding. Repeat the steps beginning with the cake. Add Cool Whip. Sprinkle coconut on top. Sprinkle nuts on top of coconut. Garnish with cherries. Serves 45.

Italian Cream Cake

CAKE

½ cup unsalted butter, softened
½ cup shortening
2 cups sugar
5 eggs, separated
1 teaspoon baking soda
2 cups all-purpose flour
1 cup buttermilk
1 teaspoon vanilla
1 can angel flake coconut
1 cup chopped walnuts

CREAM CHEESE FROSTING

1 (8 ounce) package cream cheese, softened
½ cup unsalted butter, softened
1 box powdered sugar
1 teaspoon vanilla
chopped nuts and coconut, for garnish

Preheat oven to 350 degrees. Cream butter and shortening. Add sugar. Beat until mixture is smooth. Add egg yolks and beat well. Sift together baking soda and flour. Add to creamed mixture alternately with buttermilk. Stir in vanilla, coconut and nuts. In large glass mixing bowl, beat egg whites until stiff. Fold in beaten egg whites. Pour into three 8-inch pans or two 9-inch pans and bake for 30 minutes. Let cool. For frosting, mix together cream cheese, butter, sugar and vanilla. Stack cake layers with frosting between each. Frost cake, using coconut and nuts as desired for garnish.

No Sugar Added
Low Fat Mocha Cheesecake

CRUST

44	low-fat chocolate wafer cookies, crushed
¼	cup margarine, melted

2	tablespoons unsweetened cocoa powder
¼	cup Splenda sweetener

FILLING

24	ounces low-fat cream cheese, softened
1	cup Splenda sweetener
2	eggs
2	additional egg whites
1½	tablespoons cornstarch

¼	teaspoon salt
¾	cup low-fat sour cream
2	teaspoons vanilla
1¼	teaspoons instant coffee
2	(.55 ounce) envelopes instant hot cocoa mix

Preheat oven to 400 degrees. In large mixing bowl, mix wafer cookies, margarine, cocoa and Splenda together. Press into a 9-inch springform pan. Place pan on a cookie sheet and bake for 10 minutes. Remove from oven and cool to room temperature. For filling, preheat oven to 325 degrees. In a large mixing bowl, beat cream cheese and Splenda together until well mixed and smooth. Add eggs, egg whites, cornstarch and salt. Mix until smooth. Add sour cream and vanilla. Mix until well blended. Measure ½ cup of the cheesecake batter into a separate bowl. Add instant coffee and cocoa. Mix well. Pour ½ of the plain batter over cooled crust in springform pan. Top with half of the coffee batter mixture by dropping rounded spoonfuls over the plain cheesecake batter. Using the tip of a spatula or knife, gently swirl the coffee batter into the plain batter. Repeat with remaining batters until all is in the pan. Bake 45 to 50 minutes or until center is almost set. Remove from oven and gently run a metal spatula around the rim of pan to loosen cheesecake (helps prevent cracking). Let cool 20 to 25 minutes before covering and placing in the refrigerator. Refrigerate 4 to 6 hours or overnight before serving.

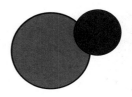

Cherry Delight

CRUST

2	cups plain flour	1	cup chopped pecans
2	sticks soft margarine		

FILLING

8	ounces cream cheese	1	package Dream Whip
2	cups powdered sugar	1	can cherry pie filling

Mix crust ingredients and put in pan; bake 15 minutes at 350 degrees; cool. For filling mix sugar and softened cream cheese well; mix Dream Whip according to directions on package, and fold into sugar and cheese mixture. Pour onto crust; cover with cherry pie filling. Keep in refrigerator.

Apple-Cranberry Crunch

	sliced apples to cover large baking dish	½	cup brown sugar
		½	cup all-purpose flour
1	can whole cranberry sauce	1	stick margarine
1	cup sugar		nuts, chopped
1	cup oats		

Preheat oven to 350 degrees. Mix apples, cranberry sauce and sugar in buttered baking dish. Mix oats, brown sugar, flour, margarine, and nuts. Cover apples and cranberry mixture with the oats mixture. Bake for about 1 hour.

Oreo Delight

½ gallon vanilla ice cream, softened
1 (16 ounce) tub Cool Whip, thawed
1 package Oreo cookies, crushed

In large bowl, mix ice cream, Cool Whip and crushed Oreos together. Pour into a 9x13-inch pan and top with additional cookies. Cover and freeze. When frozen, slice and serve.

Ice Cream Sandwich Delight

1 (12 ounce) box ice cream sandwiches
½ bag almond toffee bits
1 jar caramel topping
1 (8 ounce) tub frozen whipped topping, thawed
1 cup pecan halves, toasted
chocolate syrup

Spray a 9x13-inch dish with vegetable oil spray. Layer first 5 ingredients in the order listed, then drizzle with chocolate syrup. Cover tightly and freeze. Remove from freezer 15 to 30 minutes before serving.

Butter Pecan Ice Cream

1 cup chopped pecans
2 tablespoons butter
½ cup light brown sugar
½ cup pure maple syrup
4 eggs, beaten
1 can sweetened condensed milk
1 small box butter pecan pudding mix
1 large can evaporated milk
whole milk

Roast pecans in butter approximately 10 minutes in the oven. Cool and set aside. Using electric mixer, combine sugar, syrup, eggs, sweetened condensed milk, pudding mix, and evaporated milk. Pour into freezer canister. Add pecans and enough whole milk to fill canister. Freeze.

Buttermilk Ice Cream

2 eggs
2 cups sugar
2 cups milk

1 quart buttermilk
1 pint whipping cream
1 large can crushed pineapple

Whisk eggs and add sugar. Combine with milk in large saucepan. Cook on medium heat until thick. Allow to cool. Add buttermilk, whipping cream, and pineapple. Mix together and pour into ice cream freezer. Freeze until firm.

Easy Vanilla Ice Cream

½ gallon milk
1 (12 ounce) can evaporated milk
1 can sweetened condensed milk

½ pint whipping cream
1 cup sugar
1½ teaspoons vanilla

Mix milks, cream, sugar, and vanilla and freeze.

Milky Way Ice Cream

½ cup milk
8 Milky Way bars
5 eggs
1 cup sugar

1 can Eagle Brand milk
1 tablespoon vanilla
¼ teaspoon salt
1 quart half and half

Place candy and milk in heavy saucepan over low heat until candy is melted. Beat eggs and sugar first and then add remaining ingredients and continue beating until well mixed. Pour into ice cream freezer canister, then add enough milk until one inch from top. Place lid on firmly and freeze until firm.

Old Time Egg Custard

4-5 eggs, separated and beaten
½ cup sugar
2½ cups hot milk (do not boil)
1 teaspoon vanilla extract

¼ cup butter
dash nutmeg
dash salt
1 (8 inch) pie crust

Blend eggs with sugar, add salt and flavoring. Slowly add scalded milk while stirring. Pour custard into pastry lined pie pan. Sprinkle with nutmeg and dot with butter. Bake at 400 degrees for 25 minutes. Pie will set when cool.

Easy Cobbler

1 stick margarine
1 cup flour
1 cup sugar
1 cup milk

½ teaspoon salt
3 teaspoons baking powder
1 teaspoon vanilla extract

Put margarine in 9x13 inch pan. Place in hot oven to melt. While melting, stir together the remaining ingredients. Pour into melted margarine. Do not stir. Add sweetened fruit, such as peaches, berries or cherries. Do not stir. Just spoon over top. Bake in 350 degrees oven for 45 minutes to 1 hour.

Never Fail Pie Crust

2 teaspoons salt
1 tablespoon vinegar
1 large egg

½ cup water
4 cups unsifted flour
1¾ cups Crisco

Combine flour and Crisco until crumbly. In a small bowl beat together water, vinegar, egg and salt. Combine the 2 mixtures stirring with fork until all ingredients are moistened. Do not knead or over mix. Divide dough into 5 to 6 portions. Wrap each in plastic wrap. Chill for 30 minutes before using. The dough can be frozen for up to 3 months before use.

Amazing Coconut Pie

2   cups milk
¾   cup sugar
¾   cup biscuit mix
4   eggs

¼   cup butter, softened
1   teaspoon vanilla extract
1   cup coconut

Mix first 6 ingredients together in a blender for 3 minutes. Pour into a greased 9 inch pie pan. Let stand 5 minutes. Sprinkle 1 cup of coconut over top. Bake at 350 degrees for 40 minutes.

Buttermilk Pie

1   (10 inch) pie shell
½   cup butter, softened
2   cups sugar
3   eggs, slightly beaten
1½ teaspoons vanilla extract

1   cup buttermilk
3   tablespoons flour
¼   teaspoon lemon extract
    dash of salt

Preheat oven to 400 degrees. Cream butter and sugar; add eggs, vanilla extract, salt and lemon extract, and beat well. Add flour alternately with buttermilk; mixing well. Pour into unbaked pie shell. Bake at 400 degrees for 10 minutes, then bake at 350 degrees for 45 minutes, until lightly browned. (Use strips of foil or crust edge protectors to keep rim of pie from over-browning.)

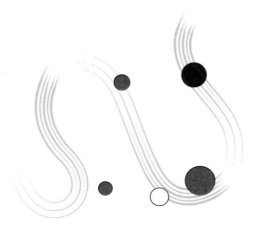

Key Lime Pie

1 small box sugar-free lime flavor gelatin
¼ cup boiling water
2 (8 ounce) container Key lime flavor light yogurt

1 (8 ounce) container frozen whipped topping, thawed
1 prepared graham cracker pie crust

Dissolve gelatin in boiling water. With wire whisk, stir in yogurt. With wooden spoon, fold in whipped topping. Pour mixture into prepared crust. Refrigerate overnight or at least 2 hours. You can also substitute sugar-free strawberry gelatin and strawberry yogurt or other combinations.

Peanut Butter Pie

½ cup margarine
1 cup flour
½ cup finely chopped roasted peanuts
1 (3 ounce) package cream cheese, softened

1 cup confectioners' sugar
½ cup crunchy peanut butter
½ cup milk
1 (8 ounce) container Cool Whip

Cut margarine into flour until crumbly, stir in nuts, press into 9-inch pie pan. Bake 20 minutes at 350 degrees. Cool completely. Beat cream cheese, sugar and peanut butter. Add milk gradually. Fold in Cool Whip and pour into crust. Cover and freeze until firm.

Pecan Pie

3 eggs
1 cup sugar
1 tablespoon flour
1 cup Karo syrup

½ stick butter or margarine
2 teaspoons vanilla extract
1½ cups pecans

Beat 3 eggs in a bowl. Add sugar and flour and continue beating. Add Karo syrup and the melted butter or margarine. Add vanilla extract and mix well. Place prepared pie crust in pie pan. Add pecans on top of the pie crust then pour syrup mixture over pecans. Bake at 375 degrees for 45 minutes.

Pumpkin Pie

2   eggs
1   pound can pumpkin
¾   cup sugar
½   teaspoon salt
1   teaspoon cinnamon

½   teaspoon nutmeg
1   small can condensed milk
¼   cup milk
2   (8 inch) pie shells

Beat eggs, add pumpkin, and sugar. Mix well. Add remaining ingredients. Pour into unbaked pie shells. Bake at 425 degrees for 15 minutes. Reduce heat, and bake at 350 degrees for 45 minutes longer. This recipe makes 2 pies.

Chocolate Fudge Pie

1   Pillsbury Ready Crust
4   tablespoons cocoa
4   tablespoons flour
1   cup sugar

2   eggs, beaten
1   teaspoon vanilla extract
½   cup margarine, melted

Mix cocoa, flour, sugar, eggs and vanilla extract. Add melted oleo. Pour into unbaked pie shell. Bake 25 minutes at 375 degrees.

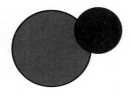

Easy Banana Pudding

1	(8 ounce) container Cool Whip	1½	cups water
1	can Eagle Brand condensed milk	36	vanilla wafers
2-3	bananas, sliced	1	package instant coconut pudding

Mix pudding with water. Fold in Cool Whip and condensed milk. Layer in trifle bowl, starting with wafers, then bananas, ending with pudding mix. Chill before serving.

Old Fashion Banana Pudding

¾	cup sugar, divided		whole milk
⅓	cup all-purpose flour	2	tablespoons margarine
	dash of salt	½	teaspoon vanilla extract
4	eggs, separated	6	bananas, really ripe
1	whole egg		vanilla wafers
1	small can evaporated milk		

Mix ½ cup sugar, flour and salt in the top of a double boiler. Stir in 4 egg yolks and 1 whole egg. Pour evaporated milk into a 2 cup measuring cup and finish filling with whole milk. Add to double boiler. Blend well. Cook over boiling water, stirring constantly, until thickened. Add margarine. Reduce heat and cook, stirring occasionally, for 5 minutes. Remove from heat and add vanilla extract. Place a small amount of the filling in the bottom of a 2 quart casserole dish. Cover the bottom of the dish with a layer of vanilla wafers. Top with 2 sliced bananas. Pour about ⅓ of the filling over the bananas. Continue to layer the wafers, bananas and filling to make 3 layers of each, ending with filling. Beat egg whites until stiff but not dry; gradually add ¼ cup sugar and beat until stiff peaks form. Spoon on top of pudding, covering entire surface and being sure to seal around edges. Bake in a preheated oven for 5 minutes or until lightly browned.

Easy Peach Dessert

1 large can sliced peaches
1 yellow cake mix
1 stick margarine

½ cup nuts
1 container whipped topping

Pour peaches and juice into bottom of 9x13 inch pan. Sprinkle dry cake mix on top. Add nuts and slice margarine over top of mixture. Bake at 350 degrees for 40 minutes.

Strawberry Pretzel Dessert

3 cups crushed pretzels
¾ cup butter, melted
2 tablespoons sugar
1 (8 ounce) package cream cheese, softened
1 cup sugar

1 (8 ounce) non-dairy whipped topping
2 (3 ounce) packages strawberry gelatin
2 cups hot water or pineapple juice
2 (10 ounce) packages frozen strawberries, partially thawed

Heat oven to 350 degrees. Combine pretzels, butter and 2 tablespoons sugar. Press into a 9x13 inch baking dish. Bake at 350 degrees for 10 minutes; cool. Beat cream cheese and 1 cup sugar until smooth. Fold in whipped topping; spread over cooled crust. Combine gelatin and hot water or juice, stir until dissolved. Refrigerate until mixture starts to set. Stir in partially thawed strawberries and pour over cream cheese. Refrigerate overnight. Cut into squares to serve. Serves 10 to 12.

Oreo Cookie Dessert

1 package Oreo cookies
4 tablespoons melted butter
½ gallon of your favorite ice cream

1 can Hershey's Chocolate Fudge Topping
1 container of Cool Whip

Smash Oreo cookies and combine with melted butter. Spread in a greased 9x13 inch baking dish. Bake for 8 minutes at 325 degrees. Cool and place in freezer for 20 minutes. Spread ice cream over crust and freeze until firm. Spread fudge topping over ice cream and freeze again for 20 minutes. Spread Cool Whip on top. Cover and store in freezer until ready to serve.

Sugar Free Apple Pie

6 cups apples, peeled, cored and thinly sliced
½ tablespoon liquid Fastsweet
2 tablespoons flour
½ teaspoon cinnamon
¼ teaspoon salt
⅛ teaspoon nutmeg
1½ tablespoons lemon juice
2 frozen pie crust

Combine all ingredients. Spoon into pie crust. Dot top with margarine. Cover with top crust. Seal edges and cut slits in top. Bake 15 minutes at 475 degrees then lower to 375 degrees. Bake until done.

Sugar Free Fried Pies

1 can pie filling (sweetened with Splenda)
⅛ cup raisins
½ teaspoon cinnamon
⅔ cup light corn syrup
1 (10 count) can non-flaky biscuits
3 tablespoons Splenda
1 tablespoon skim milk

Mix the first 4 ingredients and set aside. Roll out each biscuit to 6 to 8 inches in diameter. Place tablespoon of fruit mixture in the center of each biscuit, fold over and crimp edges with fork. In preheated 375 degrees oven, bake pies on an ungreased cookie sheet for 15 minutes. Mix Splenda and milk and drizzle over pies while they are still warm.

Sugar Free Strawberry Pie

1 small box sugar-free strawberry gelatin
3 tablespoons Splenda
2 tablespoons flour
1½ cups water
1 pint fresh strawberries
red food coloring
1 baked pie crust
Cool Whip lite

In a saucepan, mix all dry ingredients together. Add water and food coloring. Bring to a boil; cook and stir until thick. Place the strawberries in the pie crust. Pour hot mixture over the strawberries. Chill. Top with Cool Whip lite before serving.

Sugarless Cookies

3   ripe bananas, smashed
½   cup chopped walnuts or pecans
2   cups one-minute oats

1   cup raisins
½   teaspoon salt
1   teaspoon vanilla extract

Combine all ingredients, mixing well. Let batter stand for a few minutes to allow the oats to absorb some of the liquid. Drop with a teaspoon onto an ungreased cookie sheet. Bake in a preheated 350 degrees oven for 15 to 20 minutes. Loosen the cookies with a spatula. Let them cool on the cookie sheet. Makes 2 dozen cookies.

Weight Watcher Pie

2   small boxes sugar-free vanilla
     instant pudding mix
4   cups skim milk

1   tub Crystal lite lemonade mix
1   (16 ounce) lite Cool Whip
2   graham cracker pie crusts

Mix pudding and milk. Add Crystal lite and mix well. Fold in Cool Whip. Pour into pie crusts. Refrigerate.

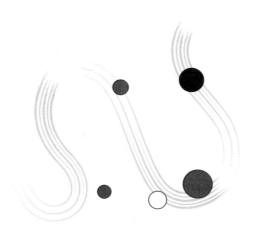

Cheese Cake Brownies

1 egg, lightly beaten	1 brownie mix
1 stick margarine	

TOPPING

1 box confectioners' sugar	1 (8 ounce) package cream cheese
3 eggs, slightly beaten	

Cream brownie mix into real soft nearly melted margarine. Add egg, spread and press into lightly greased 9x13 inch baking dish.

Topping: Mix sugar into softened cream cheese. Add eggs. Pour over cake mixture. Bake at 350 degrees about 40 minutes. Do not allow to brown, just a golden color. Cool a few minutes and cut into squares while warm.

No Bake Chocolate Cookies

1 cup milk	1½ cups crunchy peanut butter
4 cups white sugar	6 cups quick oats
8 tablespoons cocoa	2 teaspoons vanilla extract
1 stick margarine	

Bring to a boil in a large saucepan: milk, sugar, cocoa and margarine. Remove from heat. Add remaining items into the pan and stir until completely mixed. Drop by spoonfuls onto wax paper to cool. Store in airtight container. Makes 4 to 5 dozen.

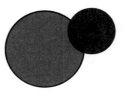

Betty's Tea Cakes

2 cups sugar
1 cup butter
2 eggs

1 tablespoon vanilla extract
½ cup milk
5 cups self-rising flour

Cream butter and sugar, add eggs and mix well. Add flavoring to mixture. Add flour and milk alternately. Ball out on floured surface, cut with biscuit cutter and place on greased cookie sheet. Bake at 375 degrees for 12 to 15 minutes.

Cornflake Cookies

1 cup White Karo Syrup
1 (14 ounce) jar creamy peanut butter

1 cup sugar
4 cups cornflakes

Bring sugar and syrup to rolling boil. Add peanut butter, stir well and pour over cornflakes. Stir until all cornflakes are covered. Dip by teaspoon onto waxed paper and let sit until cool.

Easy Peanut Butter Cookies

1 (14 ounce) can sweetened condensed milk
¾ cup peanut butter

2 cups biscuit baking mix
1 teaspoon vanilla extract
granulated sugar

Preheat oven to 375 degrees. In a large bowl, beat condensed milk and peanut better until smooth. Add biscuit baking mix and vanilla extract; mix well. Shape into 1 inch balls. Roll in sugar. Place 2 inches apart on ungreased baking sheets. Flatten with fork. Bake 6 to 8 minutes or until lightly browned. Cool. Store tightly covered at room temperature.

Chocolate Chip Cookies

2¼	cups flour	¾	cup brown sugar
1	teaspoon baking soda	1	teaspoon vanilla extract
1	teaspoon salt	½	teaspoon water
1	cup shortening	2	large eggs
¾	cup sugar	1½	cups semi-sweet chocolate chips

In medium bowl, sift the flour, baking soda, and salt. Set aside. In a large bowl, cream thoroughly the sugar, brown sugar, vanilla extract, water, and the eggs. Add flour mixture to the creamed mixture and stir well. Stir in chocolate chips. Drop by teaspoons on cookie sheet. Bake 8 to 9 minutes at 375 degrees or until just lightly browned around the edges. Cookies are best when kept refrigerated in a tin after baking.

Oatmeal Cookies

1	cup shortening	2	cups flour
1	cup brown sugar	1	teaspoon baking soda
1	cup white sugar	¼	teaspoon salt
2	eggs	3	cups oats
1	teaspoon vanilla extract	1	(12 ounce) bag chocolate chips
1½	tablespoons water	1	cup chopped pecans

Cream together shortening, brown sugar, white sugar, and eggs. Add vanilla extract and water to creamed mixture. Sift together the flour, soda and salt. Next, mix creamed mixture and sifted ingredients together then add oats, chocolate chips and pecans. Batter is very thick. Bake 10 to 15 minutes at 350 degrees.

Snickerdoodle Cookies

1½ cups sugar
2 eggs
2¾ cups flour
2 tablespoons cream of tartar

1 cup shortening
½ teaspoon salt
1 teaspoon baking soda

Mix all ingredients in order given. Chill at least 30 minutes. Roll dough in balls the size of walnuts. Roll in sugar and cinnamon mixture (2 tablespoons of each). Place cookies 2 inches apart of greased cookie sheet. Bake in preheated oven to 375 degrees for 10 minutes.

Christmas Sugar Cut Out Cookies

1 cup Crisco
2 cups sugar
6 tablespoons milk
2 teaspoons vanilla extract

3 eggs, beaten
5½ cups cake flour
1 teaspoon salt
3 teaspoons baking powder

Cream shortening and sugar. Mix vanilla extract and milk to eggs. In a large bowl mix dry ingredients together. Alternate liquid and dry ingredients with shortening and sugar mix. Mix well and chill covered overnight. Roll out dough on wax paper and cut out cookies with cookie cutters. Brush with beaten egg and decorate with color sugars. Bake on greased pan at 350 degrees for 15 minutes.

PSALMS 119:103

* How sweet are your words to my taste,
sweeter than honey to my mouth!

Buttercream Icing for Cut Out Cookies

2½ tablespoons butter, softened
1½ cups sifted confectioners' sugar
1½ tablespoons milk

½ teaspoon clear vanilla extract
¼ teaspoon almond extract

Cream butter and sugar. Add remaining ingredients until smooth. Ice cut out cookies, sprinkle with color sugars and red hots, and let stand until icing is set. I use this decorating method for the cut out cookies instead of just the color sugar.

Buckeye Cookies

1½ cups creamy peanut butter
½ cup butter, softened
1 teaspoon vanilla extract

2½ cups semi-sweet chocolate chips
2 tablespoons shortening
4 cups confectioners' sugar

You'll need wax paper, a double broiler, a cookie pan, and medium bowl. In the medium bowl, mix peanut butter, butter, vanilla extract, and confectioners' sugar (mixture will be stiff). Shape into balls and place on a pan covered with wax paper. Place into refrigerator. In a double broiler, melt chocolate and shortening. Pour into bowl and dip balls with chocolate. Refrigerate for 30 minutes until chocolate is firm.

Christmas Fruit Bark

2 (6 ounce) packages white baking chocolate squares

½ cup chopped toasted almonds
½ cup dried cranberries

Line a baking sheet with wax paper; set aside. Place white chocolate in 2 quart microwave safe glass bowl. Microwave per directions on chocolate squares packaging until chocolate is melted. Stir in almonds and cranberries. Spread on prepared baking sheet. Refrigerate until firm, then break into pieces.

Cinnamon Pecans

¼	cup evaporated milk	1	cup sugar
2	tablespoons water	1	teaspoon ground cinnamon
¼	teaspoon pure vanilla extract	3	cups pecan halves

Combine all ingredients, except pecan halves, in a saucepan, over medium heat. When sugar mixture is dissolved, add pecans and continue to cook, stirring frequently. Cook until pecans are completely sugared and no syrup is left in saucepan. Spread on wax paper to cool. Store in tightly covered container.

Peanut Butter Fudge

6	tablespoons butter	1	tablespoon vanilla extract
1	pound confectioners' sugar	4	tablespoons milk
½	cup creamy peanut butter	¼	teaspoon salt

Combine ingredients in medium bowl. Place bowl in a pan of simmering water. Stir until melted, smooth and creamy. Pour into 8x8 inch dish. Keep refrigerated. Cut into squares to serve.

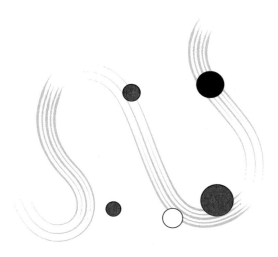

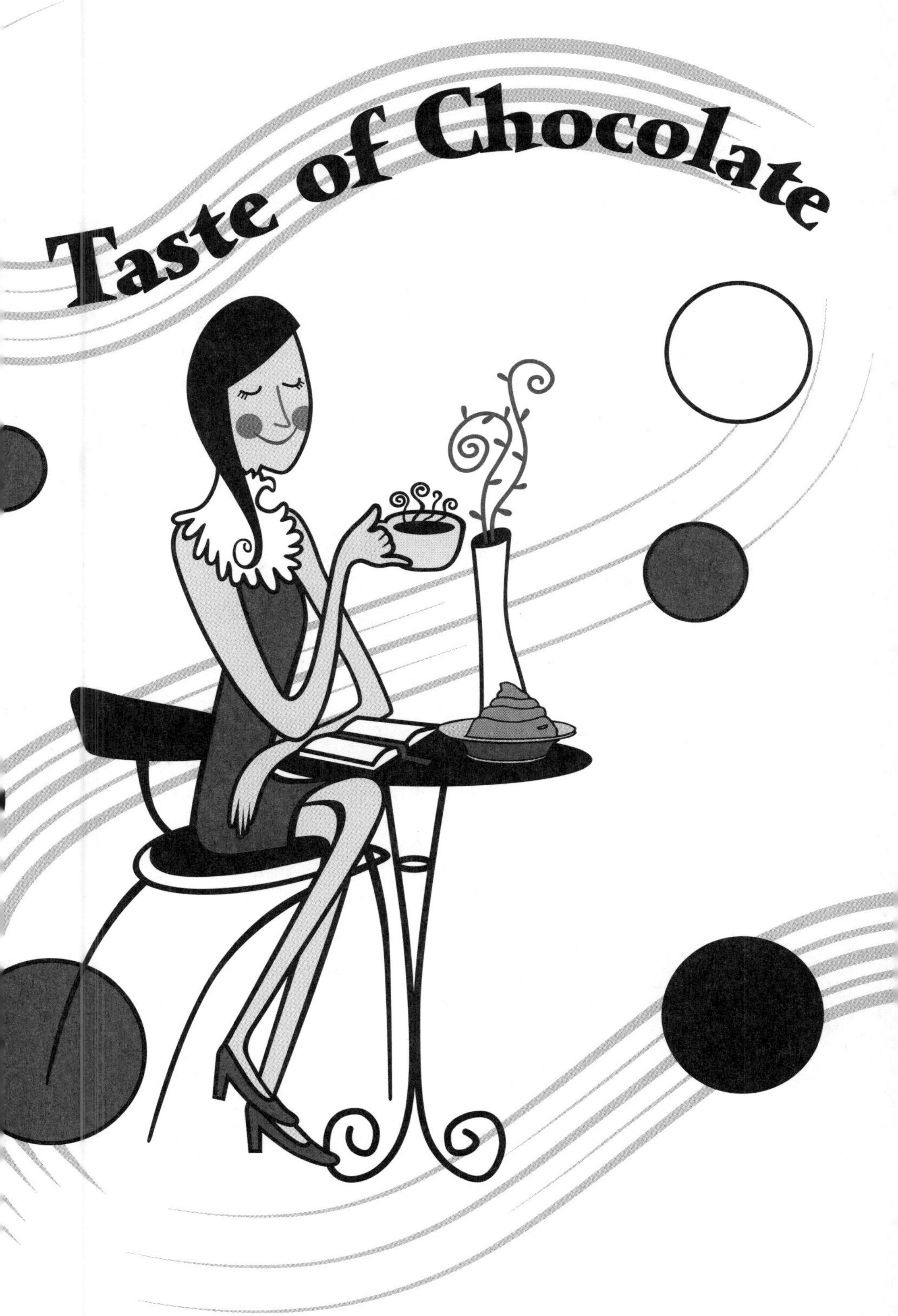
Taste of Chocolate

Fudgey Cocoa No-Bake Treats

3 cups quick-cooking rolled oats
⅔ cup creamy or crunchy peanut butter
½ cup chopped peanuts (optional)
2 cups sugar

1 stick butter or margarine
½ cup milk
⅓ cup Hershey's cocoa
2 teaspoons vanilla extract

Line cookie sheet with wax paper or foil. Measure oats, peanut butter and peanuts; set aside. Combine sugar, butter, milk and cocoa in medium saucepan. Cook over medium heat, stirring constantly, until mixture comes to a rolling boil. Remove from heat. Add oats, peanut butter, peanuts and vanilla extract. Stir quickly, mixing well. Immediately drop mixture by heaping teaspoons onto wax paper. Cool. Store in cool dry place. Makes 4 dozen.

Microwave Fudge

½ cup margarine
2 cups sugar
1 (5 ounce) can evaporated milk

2 cups small marshmallows
1 (6 ounce) package chocolate chips
1 teaspoon vanilla extract

Melt margarine, stir in sugar and milk. Cook for 7 to 10 minutes, stirring every 3 minutes to soft-ball stage. Add marshmallows, chocolate chips and vanilla extract. Stir together until smooth. Pour into a greased pan. Let cool, and then cut into squares.

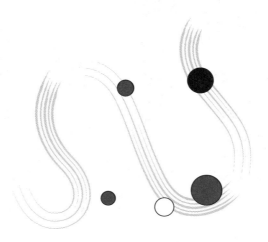

Death By Chocolate

1	box brownie mix
1	(20 ounce) container Cool Whip
9	Skor/Heath bars

1	(3.5 ounce) box instant chocolate pudding
	nuts

Mix brownies as for cake-like brownie recipe and add nuts. Bake brownies; cool. Break brownies into bite-sized pieces. Mix chocolate pudding according to directions on box. Crush candy bars and save one crushed candy bar for topping. Layer dessert as follows: ⅓ Cool Whip, ½ brownies, ½ chocolate pudding and ½ candy bars. Repeat layers and end with Cool Whip and top with one crushed candy bar.

Chocolate Lovers' Favorite Cake

1	package Devil's Food cake mix
1	(3 ounce) package instant chocolate pudding mix
2	cups sour cream

1	cup melted butter
5	eggs
1	teaspoon almond extract
2	cups semi-sweet chocolate chips

Preheat oven to 350 degrees. Grease a 10 inch Bundt pan. In large bowl, stir together cake mix and pudding mix. Make a well in the center and pour in sour cream, melted butter, eggs, and almond extract. Beat on low speed until blended. Scrape bowl and beat 4 minutes on medium speed. Blend in chocolate chips. Pour batter into prepared pan. Bake in preheated oven for 50 to 55 minutes. Let cool in pan for 10 minutes, then turn out onto wire rack and cool completely.

Chocolate Bar Cake

1   Swiss chocolate cake mix
1   (8 ounce) package cream cheese
1   cup confectioners' sugar
½   cup granulated sugar
10 (1.5 ounce) candy bars with almonds
1   (12 ounce) tub non-dairy whipped topping

Prepare cake according to package directions in 2 layers. Beat cream cheese, confectioners' sugar, and granulated sugar until creamy. Chop eight candy bars. Fold cream cheese mixture and chopped candy into whipped topping. Spread between layers and on top and sides of cake. Chop remaining 2 candy bars, sprinkle ½ on top of cake and ½ around bottom.

20 Minute Chocolate Cake

2   cups granulated sugar
2   cups flour
1   teaspoon baking soda
4   heaping tablespoons cocoa
¼   teaspoon salt
2   sticks butter
1   cup boiling water
½   cup buttermilk
2   eggs, beaten
1   teaspoon vanilla extract

Preheat oven to 350 degrees. Mix sugar, flour, baking soda, cocoa and salt. Melt 2 sticks of butter in 1 cup boiling water and pour over dry mixture. Blend until smooth. Add buttermilk, eggs and vanilla extract and mix thoroughly. Pour into greased, floured 20x16x1½ inch cooking sheet. Bake for 20 minutes.

FROSTING

1   stick butter, melted
1   (8 ounce) jar marshmallow cream
6   tablespoons evaporated milk
1   (16 ounce) box confectioners' sugar
3   tablespoons Hershey's powdered cocoa
1   cup chopped pecans

Melt butter, marshmallow cream and milk in a sauce pan, stirring constantly (mixture burns easily). Add dry ingredients and beat with electric mixer. Add pecans last and fold into frosting. Pour over cake while icing is still very hot as it gets hard quickly.

Chocolate Delight

1 cup flour
1 stick margarine
1 cup chopped pecans
1 cup Cool Whip
1 cup confectioners' sugar
1 (8 ounce) package cream cheese

1 (3 ounce) package vanilla instant pudding
1 (3 ounce) package chocolate instant pudding
3 cups milk
3 cups Cool Whip
1 Hershey bar, frozen and grated

Mix flour, margarine and chopped pecans. Spread in buttered 9x13 inch pan. Bake at 350 degrees for 20 minutes. This is the crust. Mix Cool Whip, confectioners' sugar and cream cheese. Spread over crust. Mix puddings with milk. Let set to thicken. Pour over cream cheese layer. Top with Cool Whip and sprinkle with Hershey bar. Refrigerate. Serves 10.

Chocolate Chip Cheesecake

1 cup finely ground chocolate wafer crumbs
2 tablespoons butter, softened
3 (8 ounce) packages cream cheese, softened
1 cup sugar

2 large eggs at room temperature
1 cup sour cream, room temperature
1 tablespoon vanilla extract
2 cups semi-sweet chocolate chips
¼ cup whipping cream

Lightly grease a 9 inch springform pan. Blend wafer crumbs and butter, press crumbs into bottom of pan and up the sides about 1½ inches. Beat cream cheese for 30 seconds until creamy. Add sugar and eggs one at a time, beating well. On low speed, stir in sour cream and vanilla extract. Fold in 1½ cups of chocolate chips. Pour batter into pan. Bake at 350 degrees for 40 to 45 minutes or until the cheesecake has puffed up and feels set when gently touched in the center. Turn oven off, open door slightly and leave cheesecake in oven for at least 1 hour. Remove from oven and cool. Prepare glaze by melting ½ cup chocolate chips in microwave for 1 to 2 minutes. Add whipping cream and whisk until mixed. Smooth glaze on top of cooled cheesecake. Refrigerate to allow glaze to set at least 4 hours or overnight. Remove sides of pan and cut in wedges.

Chocolate Cheese Cake

1   box Duncan Hines chocolate cake
     mix with butter
1   stick margarine, melted
4   eggs
1   box powdered sugar

1   (8 ounce) package cream cheese
     (room temperature)
4   tablespoons cocoa
½   cup chocolate chips

Mix together cake mix, margarine and one egg. Press into 9x13-inch baking dish. Set aside. Mix together remaining ingredients and pour over cake mix. Bake for 25 to 35 minutes at 350 degrees.

Hot Fudge Cake

1   box chocolate cake mix
1   can Eagle Brand condensed milk
1   can Hershey's chocolate

1   stick margarine
     vanilla ice cream

Bake cake as directed. Cut into squares and split layers. Slice ice cream and put between layers. Freeze. Cook together milk, chocolate and margarine. Boil and pour over cake squares.

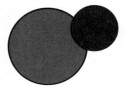

Milky Way Cake

8   Milky Way candy bars
½   cup butter
1   cup chopped nuts
1   cup shortening
1½ cups sugar
2½ cups all-purpose flour

4   eggs
½   teaspoon soda
½   teaspoon salt
2   teaspoons vanilla
1¼ cups buttermilk

Combine candy bars and butter in medium sauce pan over low heat and stir until melted. Add nuts and stir until smooth and blended. Set aside to cool. Cream shortening and sugar until light and fluffy. Add eggs one at a time. Add cooled candy mixture and mix well. Combine flour, soda, and salt. Add alternately to creamed mixture with buttermilk. Add vanilla. Bake at 350 degrees for 40 to 45 minutes.

Brownie Muffins

4   squares semi-sweet chocolate
2   sticks margarine
1   cup plain flour
1¾ cups sugar

4   large eggs
2   teaspoons vanilla
1½-2 cups nuts

Melt margarine and chocolate and cool. Mix flour and sugar; add one egg at a time to mixture, stirring as little as possible. Do not use a mixer. Add vanilla. Fold in cooled chocolate mixture and nuts. Pour into paper muffin cups until about ¾ full. Bake at 325 degrees 30 to 40 minutes. Makes 20 to 24 muffins.

Orange Brownies

BROWNIES

1½	cups all-purpose flour	4	large eggs, lightly beaten
2	cups sugar	2	teaspoons pure orange extract
1	teaspoon salt	1	teaspoon grated orange zest
1	cup butter, melted		

GLAZE

1	cup powdered sugar	1	teaspoon grated orange zest
2	tablespoons orange juice		

Preheat oven to 350 degrees. Combine flour, sugar and salt. Add butter, eggs, orange extract and orange zest. Mix until well blended. Pour batter into a greased 9x13-inch baking dish. Bake for 30 minutes or until light golden brown and set. Remove brownies from oven and pierce top with a fork. For glaze, mix powdered sugar, orange juice and orange zest until no lumps remain. Pour glaze over brownies. Cool and cut into squares. Also works well with lemon zest and lemon extract.

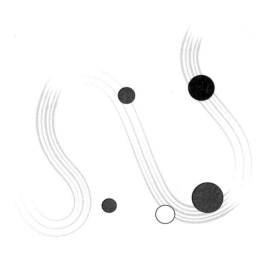

Chocolate Covered Pretzels

1 large bag of pretzels	1 pound CandiQuik (white chocolate)
1 jar salted peanuts	

Melt chocolate in container either in microwave or oven. Pour over pretzels and peanuts until well coated. Lay onto waxed paper to dry. Break into pieces and store.

Chocolate Covered Bananas

6-8 large bananas	1 tablespoon butter
½ cup chocolate chips	½ block paraffin

Melt chocolate chips, butter, and paraffin together over low heat. Slice bananas in chunks. Insert toothpicks and dip into chocolate mixture. Set on waxed paper until cool.

Chocolate Ice Cream

3 cups sugar	3 teaspoons vanilla
4 tablespoons flour	½ can chocolate syrup
5 eggs	milk

Mix sugar, flour, eggs, vanilla, and syrup. Pour into a one gallon freezer. Add milk to fill line. Freeze.

Chocolate Peanut Butter Balls

½ cup butter, softened
1 pound powdered sugar
3 cups Rice Krispies

2 cups chunky peanut butter
2 (8 ounce) Hershey chocolate bars
1 (12 ounce) chocolate chips

Mix butter and powdered sugar in large mixing bowl. Add Rice Krispies and peanut butter; mix well. Form into small balls. Set aside. Melt chocolate bars and chips in sauce pan over low heat. Dip balls into chocolate mix and put on cookie sheet with wax paper. Chill in refrigerator until set.

Chocolate Gravy

1 cup sugar
4 tablespoons cocoa

4 tablespoons flour
1 cup milk

Mix sugar, cocoa and flour together. Add milk. Cook over medium heat until thick, stirring constantly.

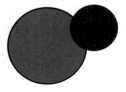

Chocolate Pizza

1	package refrigerated sugar cookie dough	½	cup semi-sweet chocolate chips
2	teaspoons butter, melted	2	tablespoons milk chocolate chips
¼	cup chocolate-hazelnut spread (recommended: Nutella)	2	tablespoons white chocolate chips
		2	tablespoons slivered almonds, toasted

Preheat oven according to cookie dough package directions. Line a heavy, large baking sheet with parchment paper. Roll out the dough to a 9-inch diameter round. Transfer the dough to the prepared baking sheet. Using your fingers, make indentations all over the dough. Brush the dough with butter, then bake until the large cookie is crisp and pale, golden brown. Remove from oven and immediately spread the chocolate-hazelnut spread over the pizza. Sprinkle the top with all three kinds of chocolate chips. Bake just until the chocolate begins to melt, about 1 minute. Sprinkle almonds over the pizza. Allow to cool approximately 10 minutes. Cut into wedges and serve.

Perfectly Chocolate Chocolate Frosting

1	stick margarine	3	cups confectioners' sugar
⅔	cup Hershey's cocoa	⅓	cup milk

Melt butter. Stir in cocoa. Alternately add confectioners' sugar and milk, beating on medium speed to spreading consistency. Add more milk, if needed. Stir in vanilla extract. Yield: about 2 cups.

Chocolate Cobbler

¾	stick butter	1	tablespoon vanilla extract
1	cup self-rising flour	½	cup milk
¾	cup sugar	1	(14 ounce) can sweetened
1	tablespoon cocoa		condensed milk

Melt butter in 8x8 inch pan in oven at 350 degrees. Mix flour, sugar, vanilla extract, milks and cocoa in small bowl. Spoon batter over butter. Do not stir.

TOPPING

1	cup sugar	1½	cups boiling water
2	tablespoons cocoa		

Sprinkle sugar and cocoa mix over batter. Pour boiling water over dry mixture. Do not stir. Bake at 350 degrees for 30 minutes. Serve with a scoop of vanilla ice cream.

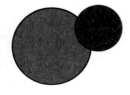

Melting Chocolate Cruise Cake

1	(11 ounce) package semi-sweet chocolate	7	eggs
1¾	sticks butter (11 ounces)	⅜	cup sugar (3 ounces)
		½	cup flour (4 ounces)

Melt chocolate and butter. Mix half of the eggs and all of the sugar. Whisk for 3 minutes and add flour. Then add the remaining egg. Add egg mixture to the melted chocolate mixture. Pour the mixture into the ramekin cups. Bake at 350 degrees for 15 to 20 minutes. Serve with vanilla ice cream. Garnish with chocolate sauce or confectioners' sugar. Best served hot.

God knew there would
be days like this.
That's why He created chocolate.

NOTES

Helpful Hints

Over-ripe bananas can be peeled and frozen in a plastic container until it's time to bake bread or cake.

When baking bread, a small dish of water in the oven will help keep the crust from getting too hard or brown.

Use shortening, not margarine or oil, to grease pans, as margarine and oil absorb more readily into the dough or batter (especially bread).

Use a metal ice tray divider to cut biscuits in a hurry. Press into the dough, and biscuits will separate at dividing lines when baked.

To make self-rising flour, mix 4 cups flour, 2 teaspoons salt, and 2 tablespoons baking powder and store in a tightly covered container.

Hot water kills yeast. One way to tell the correct temperature is to pour the water over your forearm. If you cannot feel either hot or cold, the temperature is just right.

When in doubt, always sift flour before measuring.

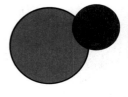

Helpful Hints

When baking in a glass pan, reduce the oven temperature by 25°.

When baking bread, you get a finer texture if you use milk.

If your biscuits are dry, it could be from too much handling, or the oven temperature may not have been hot enough.

Nut breads are better if stored 24 hours before serving.

To make bread crumbs, toast the heels of bread and chop in a blender or food processor.

Cracked eggs should not be used because they may contain bacteria.

The freshness of eggs can be tested by placing them in a large bowl of cold water; if they float, do not use them.

For a quick, low-fat crunchy topping for muffins, sprinkle the tops with Grape-Nuts cereal before baking.

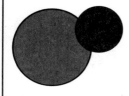

Helpful Hints

Dust a bread pan or work surface with flour by filling an empty glass salt shaker with flour.

Egg whites need to be at room temperatures for greater volume when whipped. Remember this when making meringue.

When preparing several batches of pie dough, roll dough out between sheets of plastic wrap. Stack the discs in a pizza box, and keep the box in the freezer. Pull out the required crusts as needed.

Place your pie plate on a cake stand when placing the pie dough in it and fluting the edges. The cake stand will make it easier to turn the pie plate, and you won't have to stoop over.

Many kitchen utensils can be used to make decorative pie edges. For a scalloped edge, use a spoon. Crosshatched and herringbone patterns are achieved with a fork. For a sharply pointed effect, use a can opener to cut out points around the rim.

Keep strawberries fresh for up to ten days by refrigerating them (unwashed) in an airtight container between layers of paper towels.

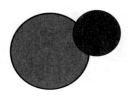

Helpful Hints

When grating citrus peel, bits of peel are often stuck in the holes of the grater. Rather than waste the peel, you can easily brush it off by using a new, clean toothbrush.

To core a pear, slice the pear in half lengthwise. Use a melon baler to cut out the central core, using a circular motion. Draw the melon baler to the top of the pear, removing the interior stem as you go.

When cutting butter into flour for pastry dough, the process is easier if you cut the butter into small pieces before adding it to the flour.

To keep the cake plate clean while frosting, slide 6-inch strips of waxed paper under each side of the cake. Once the cake is frosted and the frosting is set, pull the strips away leaving a clean plate.

When decorating a cake with chocolate, you can make a quick decorating tube. Put chocolate in a heat-safe ziploc plastic bag. Immerse in simmering water until the chocolate is melted. Snip off the tip of one corner, and squeeze the chocolate out of the bag.

Professionally decorated cakes have a silky, molten look. To get that appearance, frost your cake as usual, then use a hair dryer to blow-dry the surface until the frosting slightly melts.

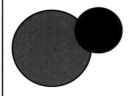

Helpful Hints

To ensure that you have equal amounts of batter in each pan when making a layered cake, use a kitchen scale to measure the weight.

Push animal shaped cookie cutter lightly into icing on cakes or cupcakes. Fill depressed outlines with chocolate icing or decorating confections.

Fill flat bottomed ice cream cones half full with cake batter and bake. Top with icing and decorating confections.

To make cookie crumbs for your recipes, put cookies into a plastic bag and run a rolling pin back and forth until they are the right size.

To decorate cookies with chocolate, place cookies on a rack over waxed paper. Dip the tines of a fork with chocolate, and wave the fork gently back and forth, making wavy lines.

A gadget that works well for decorating sugar cookies is an empty plastic thread spool. Simply press the spool into the dough, imprinting a pretty flower design.

Some holiday cookies require an indent on top to fill with jam or chocolate. Use the rounded end of a honey dipper to make the indent.

Helpful Hints

Tin coffee cans make excellent freezer containers for cookies.

If you only have one cookie sheet on hand, line it with parchment paper. While one batch is baking, load a second sheet of parchment paper to have another batch ready to bake. Cleaning is also easier.

When a recipe calls for packed brown sugar, fill the correct size measuring cup with the sugar, and then use the next smaller size cup to pack the brown sugar into its cup.

Dipping strawberries in chocolate? Stick toothpicks into the stem end of the berry. Coat the berries with chocolate, shaking off any excess. Turn the berries upside down and stick the toothpick into a block of styrofoam until the chocolate is set. The finished berries will have chocolate with no flat spots. Another easy solution is to place dipped berries dipped-side up into the holes of an egg carton.

Cut-up dried fruit sometimes sticks to the blade of your knife. To prevent this problem, coat the blade of your knife with a thin film of vegetable spray before cutting.

Cutting dessert bars is easier if you score the bars as soon as the pan comes out of the oven. When the bars cool, cut along the scored lines.

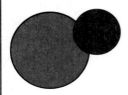

Index

D

Q

R